A fair go
Portraits of the Australian Dream

*Trixie
with best wishes
and for your memory bank
Wendy McCarthy
June 2001
Stockholm*

WENDY MCCARTHY AO

FOCUS PUBLISHING
PTY LTD

Enquiries should be addressed
to the publisher:

Focus Publishing Pty Ltd
ACN 003 600 360
PO Box 518, Edgecliff NSW 2027

Telephone: (02) 9327 4777
Fax: (02) 9362 3753
Email: focus@focus.com.au
Internet: www.focus.com.au/

Chairman: Steven Rich
Publisher: Jaqui Lane
Publishing Manager: Rod de Martin
Associate Publisher: Jennifer Walkden
Project Coordinator: Gillian Fitzgerald
Editor: Susan O'Flahertie
Production Manager: Timothy Ho
Designer: Deidre Stein

© 1999 Focus Publishing Pty Ltd

This book is copyright. Apart from any fair dealing for the purpose of private study, research, criticism or review, as permitted under the Copyright Act, no part may be reproduced by any process without written permission.

Whilst all reasonable attempts at factual accuracy have been made, Focus Publishing accepts no responsibility for any errors contained in this book.

ISBN 1 875359 56 7

Contents

Advisory Group		4
Roll of Honour		6–7
Forewords		8
Chapter One	**FIRST IMPRESSIONS** *It's about light, space and colour, the impact of different trees and landscapes, flat urban places and infinite outback horizons, new smells and new sounds.*	10
Chapter Two	**LANGUAGE** *Migrants who had a problem with language used a variety of methods to increase their knowledge and their fluency. Unhappiest were those who actually spoke English and found they didn't recognise the language Australians used.*	28
Chapter Three	**HOMESICKNESS** *Homesickness is part of the immigrant process and is usually felt most strongly in the first two years. But how could those refugees feel homesick for countries that had betrayed and abused them? The cure was to return and realise that there was no home to be homesick over.*	52
Chapter Four	**CITIZENSHIP** *Embracing Citizenship is a positive action, but if one has to give up other Citizenship, it can cause conflict within families. For some, this is the last link with the past and it is a painful subject. For others whose children have been born in Australia, the choice is made easier.*	70
Chapter Five	**WHAT DO YOU VALUE ABOUT AUSTRALIA?** *They speak of space for new ideas and new ways of doing things and say that Australians seem genuinely interested in different solutions. Physical space is also treasured: space to play, space to be creative.*	88
Chapter Six	**MULTICULTURALISM** *Multiculturalism has been a success story for more than 20 years. It embraces the best of Australian values – the right to acknowledge your cultural heritage while identifying yourself as an Australian is cherished.*	104
Chapter Seven	**IMMIGRATION** *On immigration, migrants are more cautious. Most believe the social problems which already exist should be solved before too many new migrant groups arrive.*	122
Chapter Eight	**INDIVIDUAL CONTRIBUTION** *The people who brought Asian and European expertise in food, fashion, wine and culture feel they have made strong individual contributions to Australia. But most feel their greatest contribution to Australia is their healthy, happy and well-adjusted Australian children, who will enrich Australian life with the culture they have inherited.*	136

SECTION TWO

Chapter Nine	**THE STRENGTH OF OUR DIVERSITY** *The impact that multiculturalism has had on Australian arts, culture, education and lifestyle.*	152
Chapter Ten	**THE FACTS ABOUT US** *Australia in 1999 – the statistics that define who we are and where we're going.*	164
Participants' Directory		166
Index		172
Bibliography		174

Advisory Group

Co-Patrons

His Excellency the Hon.
Sir James Gobbo AC
Governor of Victoria

His Excellency the Hon.
Gordon Samuels AC
Governor
of New South Wales

Chairman

Sir Laurence Muir
Director
Focus Publishing Pty Ltd

Zita Antonios
Race Discrimination
Commissioner
Human Rights and Equal
Opportunity Commission

Marco Belgiorno-Zegna AM
Managing Director
Transfield Investments

Anthony R. Berg AM
Managing Director
Boral Limited

Graham Bradley
Managing Director
Perpetual Trustees Australia
Limited

John Cook
Managing Director
Berri Limited

Hass Dellal OAM
Executive Director
Australian Multicultural
Foundation

Rod Eddington
Executive Chairman
Ansett Australia

Professor Stephen
FitzGerald AO
Chairman
The Asia-Australia Institute,
UNSW

Jennie George
President
Australian Council
of Trade Unions (ACTU)

Kevan Gosper AO
Vice President
International Olympic
Committee

Dr Bill Jonas AM
Aboriginal and Torres Strait
Islander Social Justice
Commissioner
Human Rights and Equal
Opportunity Commission

Sister Deirdre Jordan
AC, MBE
Chancellor
Flinders University
of South Australia

Dr Patricia Kailis AM, OBE
Director
M.G. Kailis Group
of Companies

Stepan Kerkyasharian AM
Chairman
Ethnic Affairs Commission
of New South Wales

Mary Kostakidis
News Anchor
SBS Television

Graham Kraehe
Managing Director and
Chief Executive Officer
Southcorp Limited

Jaqui Lane
Publisher and
Chief Executive Officer
Focus Publishing Pty Ltd

Tan Le
Young Australian of the Year,
1998

Nic Manikis PSM
Director
Office of Multicultural and
International Affairs, ACT

Bob Mansfield
Chairman
ComTech Communications
Limited

Nigel Milan
Managing Director
SBS Corporation

Dr Sev Ozdowski OAM
Chief Executive
Office of Multicultural and
International Affairs, SA

Sir Arvi Parbo AC
Retired Chairman
WMC Ltd, Alcoa
of Australia Ltd,
The BHP Company Ltd

Janicean Price
Director
Office of Ethnic Affairs, NT

Steven Rich
Chairman
Focus Publishing Pty Ltd

Brenda Robbins
Executive Director
Office of Citizenship and
Multicultural Interests, WA

Stefan Romaniw
Chairman
Victorian Multicultural
Commission

Vince Sorrenti
Actor/Comedian

TS Su
President
Chung Wah Association

Uri Themal OAM
Executive Director
Multicultural Affairs,
Queensland

Pera Wells
Executive Director
Federation of Ethnic
Community Councils
of Australia (FECCA)

A Note From The Publishers

We are celebrating 50 years of Australian Citizenship with this book, which is a small window indeed in the history of our vast country and in terms of its settlement by our first immigrants. However, when measured in achievements, the exponential pace of progress in Australia in the last half century is, perhaps, the most exciting since it all began. Together with our Advisory Group of prominent Australians, we commissioned our friend, Wendy McCarthy, to capture this period for us by featuring outstanding "Now Australians" who have contributed to our progress and who have seriously influenced, in their own way, the development and stature of our nation.

We are both relative newcomers to Australia. One came almost 50 years ago from the United States of America (but was born in Germany) to seek investment opportunities in this new land, and the other came from New Zealand 12 years ago to author a book about Australia's entrepreneurs.

Focus Publishing Pty Ltd began 10 years ago and we have now published more than 70 books – all featuring Australia's achievements, whether by State, by industry or through the histories of our great corporations. These books, we hope, have helped to showcase who we are as Australians and what we have built. Although some of us have been here longer than others, we have all provided depth to our national heritage; others have provided the diversity which now gives the breadth to our endeavours.

We dedicate this book to that diversity, and sincerely thank all those who have made this publication possible.

Steven Rich

Jaqui Lane

Sydney
September 1999

Roll of Honour

MAJOR PARTICIPANT

Focus Publishing

KEY PARTICIPANTS

Department of Immigration & Multicultural Affairs
Ethnic Affairs Commission of NSW
Multicultural Affairs Queensland

CONTRIBUTING PARTICIPANTS

Citibank
Commonwealth Bank of Australia
Crown Entertainment Complex
Ford Motor Company of Australia Limited
Perpetual Trustees Australia Limited
Shahin Group of Companies
TAB Limited
The Snowy Mountains Hydro-electric Authority

Forewords

A Fair Go —Wendy McCarthy

1999 marks 50 years of Australian Citizenship. Until the *Nationality and Citizenship Act* came into force, Australians were solely British subjects and had no separate Australian status. *A Fair Go* celebrates that event through the voices and experiences of 50 immigrants who arrived in Australia and have become Australian citizens.

The people selected are my choices. There are many others who could have been here. I began with people I knew and admired and followed the wisdom and advice of many who wished the project well because 'we don't celebrate our rich diversity'. In choosing people, I looked for a diverse group of individuals who collectively demonstrated a breadth of background and achievement. Individually they are leaders in a variety of situations – commerce, the professions, academia, the arts, design, development and food – to name but some. In some instances, the leadership is emerging rather than developed, and the future will decide whether the predictions are true.

This is their story and the words are theirs.

Australians are not often forthcoming with expressions of patriotism, unlike my history students in the 1960s in Pittsburgh, USA, who were vocal and forthright in expressing their love for their country and their support for the power of diversity. We take for granted what a wonderful national asset citizens such as these are. It is interesting to reflect how they may also have changed our understanding of the role of Citizenship. Certainly they have expanded the range and experience of being Australian and there can be few places in Australia without the footprint and leadership of the immigrant.

The American historian, Oscar Handlin, said: 'Once I thought to write the story of the immigrants in America. Then I realised that the immigrants were America's story.'

It is time we understood that in Australia.

An Indigenous Perspective —Aden Ridgeway

Many Aboriginal Australians have taken leadership positions by articulating their beliefs that a pluralist society can work. Aden Ridgeway, a member of the Gumbayyngirr people, is one such leader. He has played a key role in the National Indigenous Working Group and was for five years executive director with the New South Wales Aboriginal Lands Council. Recently elected to the Senate of the Australian Parliament, he is the second Indigenous person to hold Federal parliamentary office, and the first from New South Wales. He outlines his thoughts on multiculturalism.

The languages and cultures of Aboriginal Australians have flourished for at least 40,000 years. As the first Australians, Aborigines had little reason to be pleased with the white man who decimated their way of life and ignored the rich diversity of their culture. Yet, when the Europeans arrived, there was little aggression and animosity and a remarkable extent of generosity. It is an overwhelming generosity to envisage a shared future.

I belong to the school of thought that we've always been here. Certainly from my growing up, and the stories being told about our origin and existence, it was always this land and nothing else. There are no stories or evidence in the generational memory of my people that gives any credence to the concept that we came from another place. We have always been here. And that's what I believe in, and I think, in time, as science becomes more sophisticated, there will be an ability to confirm that.

Multiculturalism is important to us for it is a concept and expression of an inclusive Australian society. Indigenous people form part of that, but in a more unique and special way, being the first people and seeing themselves as always being part of, and belonging to, the land, not only in traditional terms but in contemporary standards as well.

Multiculturalism is an all-embracing way of dealing with the fact that if you want to maintain social cohesion at the national level you need to acknowledge all of the parts that make up that society, as well as recognise the unique place of Indigenous people. A nation is only whole when there is a complete recognition of the sum of all of its parts – and a small but significant part of that sum is Indigenous Australia.

We share with the post 1949 immigrants many of their concerns about language. Language needs to be maintained because it is the strongest sense of identity for most Indigenous people, particularly when they don't have access to land, to retain connection to land to reinforce identity and spirituality. Language becomes the next most important part of defining your existence and your identity.

Chapter One

First impressions

First impressions matter, and for people coming to Australia looking for a new life, whether they arrived by land or sea, these first impressions are remembered. They give a context, a sense of place to their lives. Even if there were few expectations, they were invariably measured against those first impressions.

How would Australia compare with the posters they had seen at the recruitment centres? Would it be better than Canada and the USA? Did the sun always shine? What were Australians really like? Could they love their new homeland?

Many of the people we profiled had strong first impressions. They describe physical attributes such as light, space and colour, the impact of different trees and landscapes, flat urban places and infinite outback horizons, new smells (where is the coffee?) and new sounds. These are the sensual dimensions of Australia.

The other impression is the friendliness and warmth with which Australians greeted the new arrivals; no fuss or 'no worries mate, everything will be all right'. For people whose journey from another world had often been traumatic and lonely, this laid-back approach was comforting and reassuring. There were some challenges in learning new protocols of behaviour. What did your new neighbour mean when she asked you to bring a plate? Why would you take a plate to lunch? Didn't they have enough?

The limitations of food shocked many. Where were the capsicums and spicy sausages? What did you do with a white bread sandwich and where could you find cheese? Fortunately for us, all the New Australians expanded our palates and the variety of food available to us.

The sense of space remains a powerful memory. Whether arriving at Fremantle or Port Phillip Bay by boat, disembarking at the bush railway station at Bonegilla or flying into Sydney over the harbour, that sense of light and space endures in the experience of becoming and being Australian.

Elsa Atkin

I remember being driven through the streets of Sydney and looking at the newspaper headlines to see what they were saying, and to my surprise one of them said, 'Elizabeth Taylor takes a fourth husband'. I felt, 'Wow, this is going to be very different. Fancy putting that as a news item.' It wasn't a revolution, it wasn't a royal betrayal, treason, or something like that. That was an amazing thing.

Caroline Baum

Oh beauty, just sheer beauty, and alienness. I mean, I was just completely mesmerised by colours and by gum trees, really. I was just totally fascinated by the smell and the texture and the variations of gum trees. I just went around sort of touching the barks and saying, 'God, look at this. This is a paperbark and this is a ghost gum and this is a snow gum.' I fell in love with the trees, which is kind of ironic if you think that my name means 'tree' in German. It was in Tasmania, so it was a very pure kind of Australia that I saw. I did not land in a big city.

Tim Besley

My first impression was of the bridge, which was wonderful, but it was the hugeness of Sydney. Even Wellington, which was a reasonably big city in New Zealand, is just like a village compared to Sydney. A huge mass of city. I was on my own.

Wolf Blass

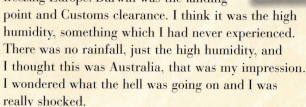

The first landing place was Darwin in January 1961. I thought I had arrived in hell because of the changeover from freezing Europe. Darwin was the landing point and Customs clearance. I think it was the high humidity, something which I had never experienced. There was no rainfall, just the high humidity, and I thought this was Australia, that was my impression. I wondered what the hell was going on and I was really shocked.

Anita Donaldson

We were in Woodside, the migrant hostel, in a Nissen hut. That summer of 1949 was dreadfully hot, and I think they had a Black Sunday in the summer of 1950, bushfires and so forth, and my family, having come from Europe, thought that this was the end of the Earth, the pits. Woodside was not exactly a fantastic place to be living in either in the middle of summer. It was quite a way from the city.

Mala Dharmananda

I remember seeing the Swan River and just being amazed at it, particularly because in India rivers are not as big and nowhere as pretty, but also, people live along the river in huts. There wasn't any of that on the Swan and it just blew me away. And there were no temples along it, it was just a river. It didn't have any religious or people connotations, but it was beautiful. That was the most overriding impression of Perth. Not the beaches. We're not a people that enjoys water culture. We don't sunbathe or anything like that. Water has always got religious connotations.

Akira Isogawa

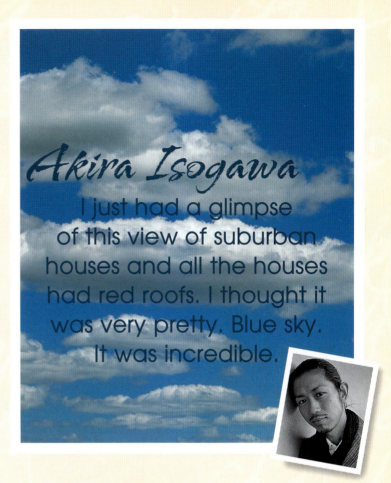

I just had a glimpse of this view of suburban houses and all the houses had red roofs. I thought it was very pretty. Blue sky. It was incredible.

Sir James Gobbo

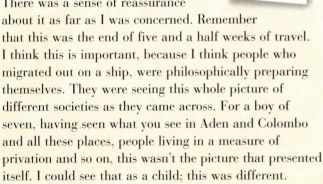

The blue sky and the sun, the wonderful light and the cheerfulness of everybody around. There was a sense of reassurance about it as far as I was concerned. Remember that this was the end of five and a half weeks of travel. I think this is important, because I think people who migrated out on a ship, were philosophically preparing themselves. They were seeing this whole picture of different societies as they came across. For a boy of seven, having seen what you see in Aden and Colombo and all these places, people living in a measure of privation and so on, this wasn't the picture that presented itself. I could see that as a child; this was different.

Bill Jegorow

It was at Fremantle and we were all very excited. The waterside workers came on board and I was working in the kitchen as an assistant – something to do on the way. I remember giving them eggs and sandwiches, which they consumed with great glee.

Ted Johnson

We landed in Adelaide to begin with, then came to Melbourne, where my father had a job lined up. My first recollection is the heat. We were certainly ill-equipped to handle that. These days they call it jetlag. I call it heatlag. It was February. It was really hot. The boat came via Perth and we landed at Fremantle for a day and that was our first sight of Australia.

Diane Grady

My first impression was this was going to be a very easy country to get used to because everybody was so nice. I mean, this idea of being met at the airport and taken out for a game of tennis was just such a friendly welcome, I guess. And you know, the city, I suppose, was physically bigger and more beautiful than I ever dreamed, and of course there were no wallabies walking down the street.

Elena Kats-Chernin

I remember my first sight of Australia very well. Very clean, little houses. It was a sunny day and I saw this little row of houses and one woman, and I still remember what she looked like. They used to call pants 'slacks'. I remember that word I had never heard before. They don't use it any more. She was wearing slacks and she was doing something in the garden and we were passing by in the car. The first couple of days we had the most amazing food, all these things that we'd never had before. We had never had toast. Or ham. It was just delicious; everything was great. I was full of optimism and positive vibrations.

Judit Korner

We arrived at this place near Maitland called Rita Camp. I was beside myself; I was hysterical because it wasn't what they told us. There weren't beautiful cottages with lovely flowers. It was hideous. I had never ever thought of myself as poor. I wasn't destitute, but this was just so heartbreakingly sad. I thought, 'Where are we? What have we done?' It certainly wasn't Vienna, it certainly wasn't Budapest or Paris. It was the back of beyond.

Vivi Germanos-Koutsounadis

They only had sandwiches on the train. Most of the Greeks didn't know what sandwiches were, so we were really getting hungry. There was somebody who spoke English and told people on the train and then they stopped at some places so that we could get some other food.

Lou Klepac

They dropped us off in Fremantle and we looked around. They put us on another train and it took five hours to get up into the bush to this military camp outside Northam, which was the most beautiful place on earth for a child my age. Hillsides covered in these pink everlastings. I thought I had gone to heaven. Parrots flying in the air. It was so beautiful. The rocks. I was looking for snakes, I was picking everything up.

Ted Kunkel

People will say Auckland is sometimes humid, but it's nothing like Brisbane. My first impression was that I had stepped into an oven. I think the second impression after that was that it was friendly. There was a warmth about it.

Nelson Leong

I was so shocked at Darwin because it was after the cyclone, so everything was on the ground. Everything was wiped out. I thought Timor was bad but this was the worst in the world. There were no houses. I had never seen a cyclone before. We don't have cyclones in Timor. The whole city was abandoned.

George Lapaine

Coming from Naples where night life is such a vibrant part of the city's life, we arrived in Melbourne in August 1951. It was pretty cold. We walked down the streets of Melbourne and there was no-one around. The pubs were closed, the restaurants were closed, no people. We really, honestly, thought there was something wrong, a plague. I remember looking around the garbage tins in the city to try and find a newspaper to see what sort of plague it was.

Tan Le

I remember peering out of the plane as we were flying into Melbourne and noticing that there was so much space and so much room in Australia. You can understand the feeling, because after five days and nights cramped up in this small little boat and three months in a refugee camp with lots and lots of people, the space was just amazing.

Dai Le

It was so hot when we got to Australia. When we got into the airport, the first impression I had – and my sister too, because we talked about it recently – was that all the people looked the same. You know, white skin and golden hair and blue coloured eyes. We were just fascinated by the fact that, to us, everybody looked the same. I suppose the Anglos look at the Asian people now and say the same.

Juliana Nkrumah

When I went into the streets I expected to see white people and Aboriginal people, but of course in New South Wales you see a lot of Asian people. I thought, 'Is this Australia?'

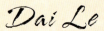

Rolando Ramos

As we stepped out of the plane in Sydney something that really made a huge impression on me was the space. The space, and somehow the cleanness of the city as well. I suppose we came from a political situation in Chile where I was feeling personally quite restricted and confined. All of a sudden that feeling was taken out of me. At the same time, physically, I could see in the environment space where you can actually live.

16 | A Fair Go – Portraits of the Australian Dream

Neville Roach

We landed at Darwin and I remember having crumbed lamb chops, which I thought were absolutely delicious. Not that I am a great fan of lamb chops, but for some reason that was a meal I do remember.

Jim Trambas
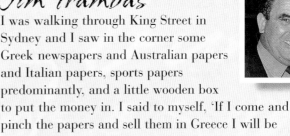
I was walking through King Street in Sydney and I saw in the corner some Greek newspapers and Australian papers and Italian papers, sports papers predominantly, and a little wooden box to put the money in. I said to myself, 'If I come and pinch the papers and sell them in Greece I will be a wealthy man.'

Paul Simons

I saw blue skies, sunshine, very laid-back people compared with what I had experienced elsewhere. I think coming from Europe, whether it was Britain or from Continental Europe as some of the immigrants did, it was war-torn. It was still run-down, it was grey and drab, there was still rationing in Britain and it was all very very depressed. And you came out here to Australia or New Zealand and both these places were impressive. The people were all very friendly. Okay they called you a Pom, or more often a Pommy Bastard, but it was done in a nice way; it wasn't derogatory.

Ngoc Trang Thomas

I arrived in October in Sydney and my first reaction was that it was cold and windy – very, very windy – and also the streets went up and down, up and down; it was very hilly. I was living in Marrickville with Colombo Plan students. We were boarding with Australian families and I was with two ladies from the Salvation Army. They brought me up, practically, and I lived with them for five years until I got married. I got married from there.

Miguel Sanz
I know that Perth looked very clean from the air and it was an unusual layout for a city, something I'd never seen before in Europe, so it looked kind of nice. They put us in this hostel, which we found out was a concentration camp, and they had lizards running underneath this camp and we found out that the reason they had these lizards was because they used to eat the snakes.

Agnes Whiten

Landing at Eagle Farm with that old Brisbane international airport, which looked like a Quonset hut, was very disappointing. Driving through the streets of Eagle Farm with these old houses I thought, 'Where am I?' I was expecting big houses and beautiful things and that was a big disappointment. After a while I was impressed because of the clean air and smooth traffic. Manila is hell with its driving. I thought the people were very friendly.

Anita Mak

My first impression of Australia was that it was much more relaxed than other places I've visited. At that stage I'd only travelled to Asian countries. There was much more space, a slower pace of life and people were easygoing and friendly. We absolutely adored Canberra; we fell in love with it straight away. It was like a big country town. I love the bushes. And we were part of a very close-knit graduate student community; we got a lot of support from people from all parts of the world.

Magda Wollner

Adelaide was a terrible disappointment because I went into a chemist shop and it reminded me of Germany. Everything was German. Even the man had a crew cut. I said to Igor, 'I don't want to buy anything', and I walked out. Then we went to Melbourne, where we actually were going to live, because we had a flat – a very lovely flat – near Toorak. I started in a sandwich shop, making sandwiches. Then I went and had another job, then another job. Then of course I knew that I was going to have to leave, because I said to myself I would never be able to hate Brisbane as much as Igor hated Melbourne. That was the deal. So we came up to Brisbane.

Ilija Kovacevic

When I arrived here it was very hard, all that red dirt and the rocks and no trees. In Europe in the big factories you have maybe 600 people or over 1000, and here every business has only one, two or three people.

Con Sciacca

I remember crying; there were so many people and my father smacked me across the bottom and told me to behave myself in the new country. We then moved to Innisfail, and one of my first real memories of being in Australia was watching the migrant women wash their clothes in the river. And worrying about somebody called 'crocodile'.

A Fair Go – Portraits of the Australian Dream

Elsa Atkin

Elsa Atkin had just finished her Catholic convent schooling and was heading to England from Bagdad to enter university, continuing the migratory tradition of most people of her Spanish-Jewish background who leave the Iraqi capital, never to return. Although they had lived in the Spanish-Jewish community of Bagdad for generations – it was, she says, a lot like Cairo or Alexandria in that lots of people migrated there and stayed within their own communities – they considered themselves westerners, and westerners never felt that Iraq was the country they belonged to.

Elsa's father died just as she was about to leave for England, and because money was tight, she was convinced by her older brother, who had recently won a lectureship at Sydney University, that Australia was the place to head. Bagdad was a difficult place to get out of, though, and when Elsa's mother requested passports for her small family group to visit Austria on the pretext of chaperoning her daughter as she moved closer to England, Bagdad's passport issuers appeared not to know that there was a difference between Austria and Australia and issued passports all round.

Since Elsa had spoken three languages since childhood, her arrival in Sydney caused no great difficulty – although she admits to warmly thanking the family's generous and welcoming first neighbours for their fantastic 'hostility'. What struck her most was a conversation she had with a clerk in a government department who was interviewing her for a job. Deep into the interview, having answered all his questions and displayed the progress she was making in her night-time university classes, she showed him her high school certificate results, which were good enough to get her into any university in England or France. Then, when she told him she was born in Bagdad, the first question he asked was whether she could speak English.

Elsa finally started her career as the personal assistant to Jorn Utzon, architect of the Sydney Opera House. She spent 10 years working in human resources at the ABC and became deputy director of the Evatt Foundation, which is involved in economic, social and political research. She joined the National Trust as Executive Director in 1994, a position she holds still.

Caroline Baum

Caroline Baum describes her parents' reaction to her migrating to Australia as 'completely scorched earth devastation'. Her mother hung the phone up in her ear each time she called, preferring to think of her as dead than living in Australia. Caroline is executive producer of ABC Radio National's *Arts Today* program. Before arriving in Australia in 1984 Caroline had a great job in London working for the BBC in arts documentary. While travelling frequently and about to be made associate producer, she met an Australian and followed him home, where they married. The child of a Jewish refugee father who had fled to England to escape persecution, and a French mother, she was a cherished only child who grew up in middle-class comfort in London in a house full of extra supplies in case of famine.

Since she arrived in Sydney in 1984 she has made a career in the arts, first as features editor of *Harpers Bazaar*, then arts editor of Melbourne's *Sunday Herald* and features editor of *Vogue Australia*. From an initial on-camera role on the ABC's *TVTV*, Caroline took on the role of presenter of the ABC book program, *Between The Lines*, interviewing literary luminaries such as Adeline Yen Mah, Margaret Atwood, Peter Carey and Ben Okri.

While racism has its well-known proponents and its victims, the difficulties of difference for the multilingual Caroline have come, strangely enough, from other Poms who believe that she can never be a real Australian while the Oxbridge plum remains in her mouth.

'It's mainly an Anglo-Irish or an Australian-Irish push that thinks that people who have this accent should not be given a voice,' she says. 'They should stay in a corner and they should not make themselves heard.'

Caroline has recently re-married another Australian and now her parents visit her every few years.

Tim Besley AO

While Tim Besley is now Chairman of the Commonwealth Bank and Chairman of the Leighton Group, he started life in Australia in 1950 as a young engineer headed for the Snowy Mountains and work on the Hydro-electric Scheme. Lured from his job in New Zealand, where he worked in the State hydro-electric design office in Wellington, by talk of wages double that which he earned in New Zealand, he had planned to stay for five years, save his money and eventually go back to New Zealand after doing a bit of travelling.

Based in Sydney until the Snowy Authority established its headquarters in Cooma, Besley was one of a group of engineers selected to travel to the United States and work with the US Bureau of Reclamation. On his return in 1953 he moved to Cooma, rising to the position of Assistant to the Commissioner (Sir William Hudson), and then transferred to the public service, joining the Department of External Territories. His rise in the public service took up most of the 1970s, and after three years in the Commonwealth Treasury, he became Secretary, Commonwealth Department of Business and Consumer Affairs and Comptroller General of Customs in 1976. He became managing director of Monier Ltd in 1982, progressing to Chairman and Chief Executive Officer. Since 1990 he has been Chairman of Leighton Holdings Ltd. He became Chairman of the Commonwealth Banking Corporation in 1988 and Chairman of the Commonwealth Bank of Australia, a position he still holds, when the Bank was privatised in 1991.

He considers his single best contribution to Australia, and certainly the most interesting for him, to be his close involvement with the bank as it was guided from wholly government ownership to private ownership, with all the attendant discussions, sometimes full and frank, with government ministers.

'I have a view that most people have some luck,' he says, 'and I think I've had all mine in the job area. It's been terrific, really. I'd certainly do it all over again.'

> 'Most people have some luck and I think I've had mine in the job area.'

Chapter One – First Impressions

Wolf Blass

Wolf Blass was an ambitious 27-year-old oenologist (wine maker) from East Germany, working as a chief wine chemist and superintendent of one of England's biggest wine importers, and wrestling with the biological disaster of German white wines transported in wooden casks and already beginning to ferment before they arrived. He dreamed of a different life and was negotiating with Australia and Venezuela. Venezuela was about to win out when revolution broke out and made up his mind for him. The South Australian Barossa Cooperative was looking for a new approach to wine making. They were looking for someone who could offer innovations to the pearl wines with which they hoped to tempt Australians away from beer.

In January 1961 Blass left below-freezing temperatures and arrived in Darwin, thinking he had landed in hell. After a couple of weeks' public relations work in Sydney, he went to Adelaide to Kaiser Stuhl Wines, a wine makers' cooperative with a million-pound debt and three hundred grape growers attached. His job was to streamline white table wine production and get into pearl wine production. Within three years, 80 per cent of all pearl wines in Australia were made by Kaiser Stuhl, including such temptations as the fruit-flavoured pearls, Pineapple Pearl and Cherry Pearl.

After introducing quality table wines into the portfolios of several wine makers, he started his own business, and soon began exporting to New Zealand, Fiji, Hong Kong, Singapore, Malaysia and Papua New Guinea.

Wolf Blass Wines became a public company in 1984, and by the end of 1990 had won 2575 national and international awards. He has been Australia's most successful red wine exhibitor at national wine shows in Sydney, Melbourne, Perth, Adelaide, Brisbane, Hobart and Canberra nine times in 10 years, and has had an enormous impact on the image and quality of Australian wine.

Paul Boyatzis

Paul Boyatzis came to Australia for a family reunion. In 1939, just as the war was starting, Boyatzis' father had left the Greek island of Castellorizo, because of the declining opportunities, and headed for Australia. The two-year-old Paul, along with his mother and grandparents, were about to join him when they were stranded by the outbreak of war. They eventually managed to leave Castellorizo when it came under German attack in 1943: the island had been under Italian administration but was liberated by the British, at which point the Germans bombs fell. Boyatzis and his family were evacuated to Cyprus and then to Palestine, then spent two years in Alexandria. The family eventually reunited in Perth in 1947.

Boyatzis Sr had chosen Australia because two of his brothers were here as well as other members of his family, and Perth already boasted a substantial population of Castellorizians.

When Paul Boyatzis stepped off the boat in Australia as one of the first mass arrivals of immigrants, he not only saw his father for the first time in memory but was also reunited with members of his extended family.

Without much schooling up to that point, and no English language, the 10-year-old tackled the Perth school system then studied medicine in Perth and Adelaide. After graduation he worked for three years at the Royal Perth Hospital, in his final year specialising in ear, nose and throat. He did postgraduate work in England in ear, nose and throat and was recruited back to Perth to a practice in which he remains, although in a different capacity.

What he values most about his great heritage is 'filotimo', a word that cannot be translated into English – but 'love of honour' gets near it. Essentially, with filotimo, a man is great; without it he is only half a man. 'Once you do something to lose your filotimo, you have lost your essence of value,' he says.

'Once you do something to lose your filotimo, you have lost your essence of value.'

Chapter One – First Impressions

Judy Cassab AO CBE

After the war, artist Judy Cassab's family escaped Hungary with a Czech passport which took them as far as Vienna. For months they sat in Viennese coffee houses twirling a globe and eliminating countries they didn't want to live in. The Hungarian quota was already full in England and in the United States, but Canada and Australia looked possible. They waited two years for their request to be answered, living in Vienna for one year and Salzburg for another where the presence of Americans made them feel safer.

From Salzburg Judy and her husband and their two children arrived in Fremantle in 1951 – on the maiden voyage of an Italian ship which had no nursery, no nurse and a lack of medical supplies. Not being able to face 10 more days on the ship they flew on to Sydney, only to be faced with a lack of coffee shops and an all-pervasive smell of dripping.

But the people were friendly, and very soon after her arrival Judy met Sheila MacDonald, who was a painter and had a studio in Phillip Street and a sketch club which Judy joined with Rapotec, a Yugoslav, George Olszansky, a Pole and a lot of Australian hobby painters.

Championed by the radio personality Andrea, Judy soon started receiving commissions to paint portraits, starting with Roy McKerihan, President of the Rural Bank. Two portraits she painted of top models, Judy Barraclough and Elaine Haxton, won 500 guineas each in the *Australian Women's Weekly* prizes of 1955 and 1956, which allowed Judy money enough to travel back to Europe to study the great paintings she missed seeing because of the war. Letters from those models to friends in London brought her more commissions there, and as more people saw her work the number of commissions snowballed. Judy soon had enough work on both sides of the world to allow her to commute between London and Sydney.

Chapter One – First Impressions | 25

Leslie Cassar AM KSJ

Although born in Alexandria, Egypt, Leslie Cassar's family had its roots in Malta. Leslie was a young teenager when his family was unceremoniously booted out of Egypt at the time of the Suez Canal crisis. Distance was a factor in the choice of Australia. His father and grandfather chose Australia, distant enough from the troubles of Europe, yet not so removed as they would feel living in Canada. Australia was a new frontier for the family, a promise that the problems they suffered during World War II would not follow them.

Settling in Melbourne, Leslie finished school in 1961 and joined Qantas as a junior commercial trainee. He held various senior appointments with the airline, ending up as general manager with responsibility for the airline's operations in Italy, Spain, Portugal, Malta, Yugoslavia, Iran and the eastern Mediterranean. Living abroad for 14 years as a Qantas manager he learned what it was he valued most about Australia. 'Our government and the freedom that government gives us,' he says. 'You realise when you live somewhere else, not when you're visiting as a tourist, but when you're living and trying to cope with the laws of different countries, how fortunate we are with the freedom of trade, the freedom of movement and the freedom of thought that we have here.'

He resigned from Qantas to become a partner and director of Concorde International Travel in Australia, a company which allied former competitors in the travel industry and grew their business to what is now an annual turnover of $1.7 billion and broadened its business to include Smartravel Solutions, providing information technology to the travel industry and major Internet service providers.

Leslie has worked over the past 24 years to develop relations between Australia and Malta, and is currently president of the Australian-Maltese Chamber of Commerce. On Australia Day in 1997 he was invested as an Officer in the General Division of the Order of Australia.

'You realise when you live somewhere else, trying to cope with the laws of different countries, how fortunate we are.'

Arlene Chai

The Chai family made a decision to come to Australia over the strong resistance of their daughter, Arlene. Her father felt that Manila was no place to be raising his children, and Arlene was young enough and unmarried enough to be caught up in the sweep of the family when they resettled in Australia in 1982.

'My father didn't think Manila was the place to raise children because the political situation wasn't great,' she says. 'There were a lot of kidnappings of Chinese at that time. There was also a lot of corruption, and I think he wanted a fresh start. We came as a family because that's a very Asian thing to do, and if you were an unmarried daughter you basically moved with your family whether you wanted to or not.'

Arlene had risen quite high in the advertising industry in Manila where she was a creative director in a big agency. She knew that coming to Australia would require her to start again, at the bottom, but her former boss arranged a job for her with a sister agency in Sydney, where she started as a copywriter. The author of the books *Eating Fire and Drinking Water*, *The Last Time I Saw Mother* and *On The Goddess Rock*, Arlene says she values Australia because of the sense of freedom she has and the belief that she can be what she wants. 'I know this is strange, but the sense of space is so different,' she says. 'In Manila it's so congested, there are so many people that it affects the way you think as well. But here it's all about space, and I think that frees up your mind and so you start thinking of possibilities in your life. If I had stayed on in Manila I would never have left advertising and started writing books. I wouldn't have done it because that would not have been an acceptable career path. But here it is.'

Chapter Two
Language

The first European immigrants had great difficulty communicating with Aboriginal Australians. Convinced of the superiority of their mother tongue, English, they thought those who did not speak it to be heathens and savages. Few English speakers attempted to study Aboriginal dialects, and this caused great hardship to Aboriginal people and seemed to confirm their inferior position. Similarly, the Chinese immigrants of the 1800s were locked out of formal communication unless they learned English.

As the British Empire spread, so did the dominance of English.

English became the language of Australia. It was not surprising, therefore, that English-speaking migrants were preferred. It was easier and, rightly or wrongly, common values were assumed. Language was the metaphor for the main premise of the immigration program; newcomers had to adopt the Australian way of doing things. This was not a melting pot version of immigration, along the lines of the American model, but a program where immigrants turned into Australians.

This was to be done with as little interference from government as possible. It was assumed that people would want to become Australians and we were doing people a favour in rescuing them from poverty.

The post-1949 immigration policy of recruiting from non-English speaking backgrounds presented official policy-makers with language challenges. Instruction in English, whether it was provided before or during the journey, upon arrival or made available through ongoing programs, was given mainly to assist transition into the workforce. This could be justified to the Australian community as being essential and practical, and helped the obvious differences disappear.

For many families, language remained a barrier, and this was particularly true for the women who were trying to manage families, often with meagre resources and without extended family support. In many cases they wanted to keep their first language and ensure that their children became bilingual. Sadly, some became isolated as their children embraced English and could not share their parents' stories about their past lives.

It also meant that their contribution to Australia was undervalued. Unable to communicate effectively, many of the first generation of women remain the unsung heroines of the post-1949 immigration. Within even this small sample, there are examples of brides as young as 16 arriving to marry 18-year-old husbands with no English. Yet they nurtured and grew their families and had satisfaction from that.

By the 1970s the science of teaching English as a second language had developed. We recognised that language was the key to providing entry into Australian life and that to lack facility in English was to risk long-term difficulties.

Elena Atkin

I was brought up speaking three languages right from when I was a kid. I spoke French, English and Arabic right from the beginning of my life. I also took on German and Italian when I was a teenager, just because I am so interested in languages.
I remember my mum saying to me, 'This is so wonderful. Thank them. They are just so generous.' I said, 'Mum would like me to thank you from the bottom of my heart for your fantastic "hostility".'

Judy Cassab

I was very lucky because most immigrants who get into a profession, say like the rag trade, they can speak very well about the rag trade but not about other things. Because I painted portraits of people in very very different backgrounds like, for instance, the Chairman of Smith's potato chips who was a cultured, wonderful, English gentleman who built church organs in England before he emigrated, God knows why, and here he almost starved because nobody wanted what he could do and so he boiled oil on the street and put potatoes in and became a millionaire. Then I painted Sir John Eckers, who was a Nobel Prize winner and a scientist in Canberra who took me to his laboratory. So it was not only one thing that I was having conversations about.

Caroline Baum

Well I suppose one person sticks out as being a really perverse mentioner of language and that is a Pom. A zealous Pom convert who has become an Australian, like I have, but somehow thinks that because I have got this Oxbridge, plummy accent as opposed to a regional accent I can never make the grade. I can never be Australian enough even for someone who is a Pom.

Les Cassar

My mother had always insisted that we speak French at home and we'd been to a private English school in Alexandria. We had an accent and that was something you couldn't have in 1956. I was put into a Catholic college in Melbourne. I had a hard time initially, I had to get rid of that accent and I think a lot of it has stayed with me. But what was instilled in us straight away was that we had a new life and we had to perform, I guess, to make sure that we succeeded.

Paul Boyatzis

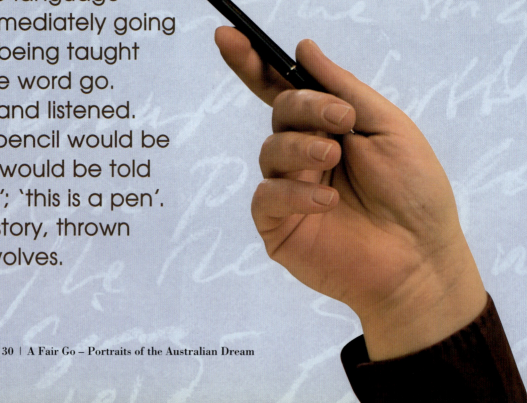

I overcame the language problem by immediately going to school and being taught English from the word go. I just sat there and listened. Periodically a pencil would be lifted up and I would be told 'this is a pencil'; 'this is a pen'. It was the old story, thrown amongst the wolves.

Josef Chromy

Certainly I didn't know any language other than Czech and Russian, which I had to learn at school, a little bit of Russian, so I had the trouble of learning English and so on. Maybe it was a bit more trouble than it should be because I was always working two jobs, or long hours, so I learned mainly just by talking and not by learning. I did a little bit of correspondence school but I got every bit of overtime I could, so it was a bit slower.

Mala Dharmananda

There were huge nuances. We spoke with very strong Indian accents and I had to go to elocution lessons to learn to speak slowly and to be understood. Our written English wasn't a problem but I think all of us had strong Indian accents, which now we don't really have. That was hard work. And people did comment on the way we spoke English. I remember my parents being mortified when, soon after we arrived here, we were invited to a barbecue and they said, 'bring a plate'. My mother took six empty plates and she kept saying to my father, 'Are you sure they don't have enough plates?' So we turned up with our empty plates. Now you can look back and laugh but my parents must have been mortified because they didn't understand. And they don't explain those things, do they?
And BYO was another thing we didn't understand.

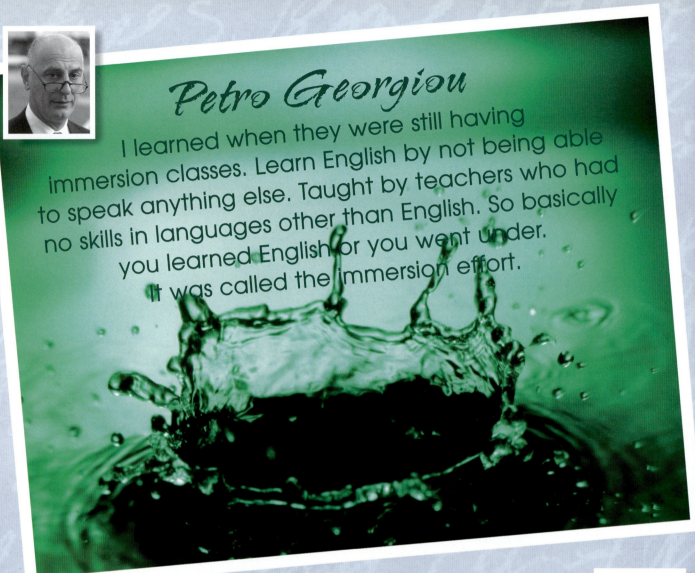

Petro Georgiou

I learned when they were still having immersion classes. Learn English by not being able to speak anything else. Taught by teachers who had no skills in languages other than English. So basically you learned English or you went under. It was called the immersion effort.

Sir James Gobbo

My parents learned a smattering, but basically it got to a stage when we learnt it that we were doing the interpreting for them. Oddly enough, that turned out to be an advantage. I thought it was terrible because I couldn't bring my school friends home because my parents couldn't communicate and it seemed all a bit different. Also, incidentally, a professor of linguistics said to me recently, 'You speak English well, you know, and you obviously didn't learn it from your parents. I come across immigrants who learn English from their parents at home and they speak a very bad English. They speak a kind of caricature of English.'

Bill Jegorow

I had learned English in Germany. But I must say that for the first six months or so, the spoken word just rolled over me like a wave over a surfer. Then suddenly I was able to understand what was said, and I started feeling pretty much at home.

Ted Johnson

I got some funny wisecracks about my accent but never to a point where you would get a racial vilification committee onto it. Nothing like that.

Elena Kats-Chernin

Language was difficult. My parents were very determined people, my Mum especially. She wouldn't let my father go out the door, she said 'no, we have to study English, we don't go out anywhere'. My mum is very disciplined; she pushed him. The funniest thing with language, when my father didn't understand everything he would come into the vegetable shop and say 'I would like 2 kilos of choice', which is what he thought the vegetables were called.

Lou Klepac

I heard Dylan Thomas and I thought, 'I want to speak like that.' I got the records and every day for about three years I listened to Dylan Thomas reciting his own poetry. He taught me to speak English more than the people around me. I wanted to speak from the gut and everyone else spoke from the mouth. I didn't want to speak just from the mouth. I mean I could, but it didn't sound right. I wanted to sound like Dylan Thomas and I always have.

Vivi Germanos-Koutsounadis

My parents couldn't go to English classes because the English class was 7.00am to 9.00am and they woke up at 6.00 in the morning to go to work and they worked overtime, up to 5.00pm and so on. They came home and they had to cook and wash and prepare the food, prepare the children, prepare the food for the next day. The next day they were up again. It just went on and on and on.

Ted Kunkel

That's the only bit I've got left. I don't know where my accent is. It is somewhere between New Zealand, Australia and Canada. It's just to the west of the Fiji Islands at the moment, I think.

George Lapaine
English? None whatsoever, apart from about four words I picked up during the American invasion of Italy, like 'okay', 'chewing gum', 'no' and 'yes'.

Tan Le
I was going to primary school and my mother realised she couldn't give me any guidance if she didn't understand Australia, so she took up night lessons in English and she would study, pasting little quotes on her machine at the factory she worked at. People at work would say, 'Why are you learning like that? You're going to be here at the factory for the rest of your life, why do you bother learning English?' The determination and willpower of people coming from somewhere else makes a huge difference. We risked our lives to come to Australia, and we were not just going to let it be.

Dai Le

We were lucky because in the Hong Kong camps there were a few missionaries who came and taught us so we knew a few words of English. That helped us, I think. Plus when we first arrived there wasn't a huge population of Vietnamese, especially in Wollongong, so we were forced to be actually part of the whole community right away, with Australians of Italian background, or Scottish background.

Mark Leibler
My parents spoke English. I'm told that when I was two years old I used to speak French. My parents spoke a lot of Yiddish at home, which I picked up.

Nelson Leong
I remember the first day we only knew 'hello'. When the teacher said, 'Sit down', we stood up, and when she said, 'Stand up', we sat down. We were confused. I think it wasn't only the language; I was confused with everything. I was in the school only for about a year or two and then they put me in the high school. That was even worse. I found out in Australia it goes by age and I was 14, so they put me in Year 10. I couldn't even write the ABC properly and they put me in Year 10. I think that was a mistake.

Ilija Kovacevic

I can talk, but writing is difficult but I'm trying every night to do some writing. With classes you have to be there every time. If you miss two weeks it's hard. But going every time and listening helps. The teacher there is very nice. I have to finish 39 subjects to collect 39 points to finish the course. I think another two years should be okay. I put more pressure this semester coming. Starting next week I will do three nights and half a day.

Satendra Nandan

English is not my mother tongue. I learnt it at the age of 14 but it's become a great instrument for exploring my own life, giving definition to my life. English has become a wonderful gift, I think, to myself and my children. How you see yourself is very important.

Juliana Nkrumah

When I tried to contact the International Students Unit for help for wives of students from overseas, the thing I was presented with was English language classes. I said, 'Thank you very much but English is my first language.' Language was no problem at all, but I found the language in the factory quite offensive.

Rolando Ramos

I had limited English at that time and trying to communicate and understand was hard. It was easier to understand sometimes, to hear and know what the other person was saying, but then to communicate back and say 'I understand' ... sometimes what I understood was totally different to what he was saying.

Gladys Roach
I remember quite clearly not understanding a word that was being said to me because, even though everyone spoke English, and I thought I did, it is amazing how the accent is. I guess it gets more pronounced in Adelaide and I couldn't understand most of what was said.

Dagmar Schmidmaier
My cousin said to me that I was just out in the street playing with the other children and within no time I was speaking English. I was four when I came, so I started school the following year and was speaking English when I went to school. We were the only children who had odd names at that school; there were no other migrant children there at all.

Sarina Russo
Because I didn't have a grip of the English language, all my other subjects were affected: my English, my history. I remember going from one neighbourhood to another just trying to get some of my neighbours to help me with my homework because I never got that at home.

Fred Shahin
I could not understand a lot of the Australian accent. I could pick a few words. It wasn't a long-term problem. It was a problem for the first year.

Ngoc Trang Thomas
I only had school English, so I could read okay, but listening to the Australian accent was a nightmare. Even for the first two years at university I really had problems understanding the lecturers. But I could read and I relied on text books.

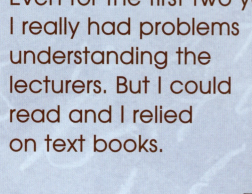

Kostya Tszyu

I learned English mainly with my trainer, John Lewis. I spent every day training and he understood me somehow. I mean, in this profession, it is easy, because it is just the basic things, like a jab. Everyone knows this kind of thing. Of course when I was relaxing, I would look at television and I concentrated on what they were talking about. It just came, I don't know how. Now sometimes I think in English and talk to myself in English.

Wolf Blass

Language wasn't an issue. In Germany, if you go to high school, I think English is the first language. The first thing I did was get myself a television to listen to *Hancock's Half Hour* and all these programs I loved.

Arlene Chai

English was my first language, so that was never a problem. It's strange growing up in Manila. You actually have three first languages; you learn them simultaneously. I speak Tagalog as well and my Chinese is not so good but I can manage. You learn them at the same time. I think in English.

Anita Donaldson

Language wasn't a problem for me because I would have gone to school with some English, but not a huge amount. My parents both became quite fluent, particularly my mother, who later on became a school teacher in Maths and Science at high school. She was trained as a dental surgeon, but when she came here she would have had to re-study for three years for a dental degree. We were a young family struggling to make ends meet. The building trade was reasonable, but not lucrative, for my father at least, so there was no way she could re-study.

Akira Isogawa

I was fortunate because I had close friends who were very patient. One of my flatmates was my English teacher, and she was great.

Sir Arvi Parbo

After the war in Germany the American army used to issue its soldiers pocket books which were literally books of a size which they could put in the back pocket of their trousers. There were books of all kinds, some of them very good books, from the classics right down to modern fiction and even non-fiction. The soldiers, when they had read them, didn't keep them; they just threw them away. So I used to pick them up and I used to practise my English by reading them.

Judit Korner

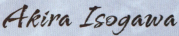

My mother was sick in the hospital on the ship all the way to Australia so I was this little kid, on my own, learning English for the new country.

Jim Trambas

I had just come out of national service and I was about 22 years of age. I was excited about coming and worried a little bit. The language wasn't an obstacle because I had enough education to be able to learn very quickly, but it was curiosity, excitement and maybe a little bit of a scare in the background. You know, the fear of failure, maybe.

Wilson Wu

English was not a problem for us as we had learned it, having been to religious-based schools, both my wife and I, in Malaysia.

Miguel Sanz

I had no English at all. I found school rather unusual because they played cricket, which I had never seen before, and they played football with this silly-looking ball which wasn't round and didn't bounce the proper way. They used to wear socks up to here, and shorts up to here. I found the whole thing rather funny. I also found in my early days that the boys always used to be together with the boys and the girls with the girls. I could never understand it, because my upbringing was to be with girls. So there was a bit of dislike because I always used to sit with the girls and because I didn't speak English it was an unusual thing for them, I guess.

Josef Chromy AO

When Stalin followed Hitler into Czechoslovakia it proved too much for 19-year-old master butcher, Josef Chromy. Without telling his family, he and two friends escaped across the border into Russian-occupied Austria on foot, then crept aboard a train to Vienna. His friends were caught and jailed but Josef was successful, evading the suspicion his lack of German would cause the train guards by first pretending to be asleep and then opting for a deaf and dumb routine. In Austria he found that opportunities weren't much better, and five hungry months later he got permission to migrate. He had a choice of going to the United States, New Zealand, Canada or Australia and chose Australia because of its distance from communism.

He was totally penniless when he arrived, and soon after, needing money to spend on clothing, he left the Bonegilla camp near Albury and headed for Tasmania, where there were jobs with long hours and overtime. He landed a job at Goliath Cement and augmented his income by working a series of part-time labouring jobs as well in his spare time. He eventually put together enough money to start a small butcher's shop and smallgoods plant at Burnie, on Tasmania's northwest coast. He called it Continental Butchers, but soon changed it to Blue Ribbon Meat Products, which was incorporated in 1965.

'I started a little business which was a little butcher's shop making smallgoods behind it,' he says. 'Then that grew until I had 18 butcher's shops. I don't have them any more because the butcher's shops were taken over by the supermarkets. I started to make smallgoods in Burnie and then in Launceston and Hobart. At that time there were about seven smallgoods manufacturers; then there were about seven exporters of the meat and I started to export. I had no customers, no suppliers and no stock, and was very much under-financed. However, I survived.'

Survival took some doing, but Blue Ribbon eventually became the largest private company in Tasmania, with 500 employees. Josef eventually listed the company, sold 70 per cent of it and invested in the wine industry, buying three vineyards and establishing a fourth at Kayena in the Tamar Valley.

In 1998 he sold the majority of his wine interests to Pipers Brook Vineyard but kept Kayena and renamed the business Tamar Ridge Wines. He now has 30 hectares planted, with plans to increase this to 55 hectares by the end of the year 2000.

Mala Dharmananda

The Malaysian riots of 1969 forced Mala Dharmananda's family to flee Malaysia and migrate to avoid living in what her father feared would be an Islamic state. As Indians and Hindus, they initially returned to India, but the war with Pakistan and Mala's mother's asthma combined to decree that the family would eventually settle in either Canada or Australia. Mala distinctly remembers voting for Australia in hopes that she'd see a kangaroo. Because Mala's aunt had already migrated to Australia and her uncles had been through the Australian university system, the Dharmanandas eventually chose Australia, arriving in 1973 and settling in Perth because of the weather.

Not long after they arrived, Australia erupted in its own form of unrest when the Whitlam government was unceremoniously dumped and constitutional crisis threatened; for a while, the political stability so important to the Dharmanandas looked extremely shaky.

'Does multiculturalism mean you can wear a sari and go shopping? Is it a signifier of culture or do you wear a sari with a dot on your head because it signifies religion? Where is the space for religion? Culture can be produced and consumed in terms of food or dance, but religion can't be consumed, and religion is a far greater signifier of identity.'

Mala spent a couple of weeks in a co-ed primary school, enough time for her to decide that boarding school back in India would be infinitely preferable, but a move to the Methodist Ladies College in Perth and a headmaster who made a huge effort to accommodate Mala and her sister in terms of their religion and their culture made all the difference. Mala went on to the University of Western Australia to get a degree in Arts then a Masters in Philosophy and is now manager of policy and evaluation with the Equal Opportunity Commission.

On increasing immigration levels for Australia, Mala questions the criteria for entry.

'Australia will accept university degrees from Britain, Canada or America, even if they're not in the top league, but they won't accept qualifications from top universities in India,' she says. 'What's the basis for that? Even if they do come here, have a look at the consultants. How many black consultants are there in radiology or surgery in private practice?'

Mala has difficulty with the concept of multiculturalism because, she feels, it camouflages a number of complicated emotive issues, among them ethnicity and religion, and for which, she feels, there is little space in Australian public discourse.

'Does multiculturalism mean you can wear a sari and go shopping?' she asks. 'Is it a signifier of culture or do you wear a sari with a dot on your head because it signifies religion? Where is the space for religion? Culture can be produced and consumed in terms of food or dance, but religion can't be consumed, and religion is a far greater signifier of identity. I don't feel multiculturalism allows me to be all I am because the word culture has so many different connotations.'

Mala feels pluralism is a concept that gives a more direct acknowledgment of the issues of race.

'There are huge problems with actually living in a multicultural society,' she says, 'because there is always the assumption that we are an homogenous group, that we have a fixed position, that we are almost tribal in that sense. But we're not. We're a fluid culture, we're diverse within ourselves, we're from different standpoints about a whole range of issues and we would like to move between two or more cultures as cosmopolitan people with a practical understanding of all the subtleties and mores of different ways of life.'

Dr Anita Donaldson

Anita Donaldson's parents fled Latvia in 1944, going first to Germany and then to Naples. From Naples they planned eventually to go to the United States, where their relatives were headed, but at the last moment, Anita's father decided on Argentina. Quite why that became Australia no-one really knows, but the family felt that there were better opportunities; and besides, if there was a ship, and you could get on it, you did, just to get away from Europe. Their ship was bound for Australia.

The family arrived in Adelaide in the middle of a heatwave in 1949 and found themselves living in a Nissen hut at the migrant hostel in Woodside, miles from the city and surrounded by bushfires.

Growing up in Adelaide, Anita wanted to become a school teacher and, for reasons she can't quite recall, it was important that she teach physical education. A Diploma of Teaching, a Bachelor of Arts and a Diploma in Physical Education combined to direct her career into physical education and dance, and she now is Dean of the Elder Conservatorium, School of Performing Arts, at the University of Adelaide.

Anita has lived as part of the multicultural experience and thinks it an important aspect of any community.

'I think there is an obligation to become a part of the community as much as you are able,' she says. 'At the same time, I think it is important not to lose entirely who you are and what you are in terms of cultural background. The difficulty is in balancing the two. I have difficulty with European people who have spent most of their lives here and can't speak, read or understand English.' She mentions the fraternities and sororities, the Saturday morning schools and folk dancing groups that Latvians set up in Australia. These organisations enable people to keep Latvian traditions alive.

'I always enjoyed it,' she says. 'I loved the folk dancing and I enjoyed the company of my peers.'

Petro Georgiou MP

Federal MP Petro Georgiou was born in Corfu in Greece. He arrived in Australia in 1951 with his parents, who felt the country would provide a good education for their children and the opportunity for personal achievement with hard work.

Petro worked hard and was rewarded for his efforts. After achieving a first class honours degree in political science at the University of Melbourne, he joined the staff of Prime Minister Malcolm Fraser. He later played a major role in the establishment of Multicultural TV, and was head of the Australian Institute of Multicultural Affairs. By 1989, Petro was State Director of the Victorian division of the Liberal Party and, in 1994, was elected to the blue ribbon Liberal seat of Kooyong in Melbourne.

Petro was four when he arrived in Australia, and remembers disembarking at Station Pier in Melbourne. As a post-war migrant, he recalls that his migrant experience was easier than that of those who arrived before the war, especially those from southern Europe.

'When I went to school I was not isolated in the school population,' he says. 'There were lots of children in similar circumstances, and we were not afraid to stand up for ourselves. Circumstances are generally better for migrants today than they have been in the past. Today for many in Australia, migrants have always been part of the scenery; it's a generational thing. Now when you observe children in school, most are relatively oblivious to cultural differences.

'It touches me personally that when large numbers of Vietnamese refugees arrived here, the reaction of most Australians was: "Well, we are doing the right thing."

It reflected a unique aspect of Australian society that constantly reassures the pessimistic side of me.

Australian immigration has been a success story. In a sense, it has come to reflect and embrace some of the best characteristics of what Australia is today.'

Vivi Germanos-Koutsounadis OAM

Vivi Germanos-Koutsounadis was born in Chios in Greece and emigrated to Australia in 1954 along with her parents and two brothers. Her seaman father was accustomed to being away at sea for long stretches of time, which left her mother alone to care for three small children. When the opportunity to emigrate came up, the family decided to leave and give the children a better education.

Her uncle owned a shop in Redfern, so when they arrived in Sydney her father went to work there and her mother took a job in a factory preparing biscuits for the Melbourne Olympics. Her parents being too busy to go to English classes, it fell on the young schoolgirl Vivi and her brothers to pick up the language and act as interpreters as well as take the responsibility for looking after six children, taking them to school in the mornings and picking them up in the afternoons.

'I think all of that had an effect on me, because I thought, why should people suffer like that? Quite often we used to go to the doctors to interpret for the people. We used to go to solicitors when people had problems with

work, also to the factories when they had problems in the work environment. They didn't know about unions and the unions weren't very interested in migrant workers.'

When Vivi's father bought a milk bar in the inner Sydney suburb of Redfern, it was to help the youngsters educate themselves. Vivi's headmistress at the time suggested that since she had a nice personality she would be better off working in her father's shop than pursuing an education. Fortunately for Vivi, her stint at a business college brought her into contact with a teacher who steered her in the right direction. Initially enrolling in a BA course because she wanted to be a teacher, she changed her mind when she realised she wanted to do something which would better the conditions of migrant people. In 1970 she graduated with a Diploma in Psychology, then found her sex and her accent were impediments to finding a job as a psychologist.

While her first job was as a probation officer for the Department of Corrective Services, Vivi became more and more involved in the pioneering of migrant services, including SBS television and radio, the Ethnic Communities Council of New South Wales, the Federation of Ethnic Communities Council of Australia and the Ethnic Affairs Commission of New South Wales. She was also heavily involved with the Greek Orthodox Community of New South Wales, of which she is now the vice president. She became a welfare worker and coordinator of the meals on wheels service for the City of Sydney Council, an Aboriginal welfare officer, a Grant in Aid Worker with South Sydney Community Aid in Redfern and, finally, in 1982, Executive Director of the Ethnic Child Care, Family and Community Services Cooperative. In this role she has been involved with developing government policy on Children's Services and Early Childhood and Child Care. She has also liaised and worked with ethnic and general peak State and national children's services organisations, lobbying for resources, policies and programs which are accessible and relevant to a diverse multicultural society.

Sir James Gobbo AC

Although Victorian Governor Sir James Gobbo was born in Australia and technically is not a migrant, his parents went back to Italy in 1934, taking their three-year-old son with them. When they decided to try again and returned to Australia, young James was seven and had no recollection of the land, nor of the language of his birth.

His first impressions of Australia were the blue sky and the sun, the wonderful light and the cheerfulness of everybody around. 'There was a sense of reassurance about it as far as I was concerned,' he says. 'Remember that this was at the end of five and half weeks of travel. I think this is important, because I think people who migrated out on a ship were philosophically preparing themselves. They were seeing this whole picture of different societies as they came across. For a boy of seven, having seen what you see in Aden and Colombo and all these places – people living in a measure of privation and so on – this wasn't the picture that presented itself. I could see that as a child; this was different.'

James completed his schooling at St Joseph's Geelong and North Melbourne and then, because his parents lived above a restaurant which made study difficult, he became a boarder at Xavier College. He graduated in Arts from Melbourne University and in 1951 was awarded a Rhodes Scholarship to Oxford. There he studied law and rowed in the Oxford University crew which won the 100th Oxford–Cambridge Boat Race. When he returned to Melbourne he practised as a barrister, and in 1978 he was appointed to the Supreme Court. He received his knighthood in 1982 for services to the community and was honoured for his service to the law, multicultural affairs and hospitals by the award of Companion of the Order of Australia in 1993. He retired from the Court in 1994; in 1995 Sir James was appointed Lieutenant-Governor of Victoria.

His parents valued the sense of opportunity and egalitarianism that Australia offered.

'We wouldn't perhaps call it a fair go, but a sense of being able to make one's way in any field,' he says. 'There wasn't any sense of your progress depending on what your family connections were. They had a sense of satisfaction that they had done it with their own hard work and that Australia was a generous country that allowed hard work to prosper and to be rewarded. That wasn't always true of the old world.'

Sir James believes that the greatest benefit of migration is the constant vitality of new people who are determined to succeed.

'I think we need the successive waves of people who come here with a hunger to succeed, with new skills, new talents and, above all, a desire to get on, a desire to advance their children and to achieve in educational and other terms. It's like getting a national transfusion every few years.

'I think people who turn the tap off on immigration just don't begin to understand the value of that, especially in a society like Australia, which is inclined to settle on a way of life that is comfortable and relaxed,' he adds.

Diane Grady

Despite having an impressive contact list, when Diane Grady went looking for a job as a journalist at *Time Magazine* she bypassed the pictures editor, who was her boyfriend's sister, and fronted up to the Personnel department. It just didn't seem right to use her contacts for personal issues.

When the Arizona-born American decided she was good at languages, she chose to study Chinese at the East–West Centre at the University of Hawaii, a facility that eventually got her working in Taiwan as a journalist on *Echo* magazine, a journal devoted to capturing the essence of Chinese culture before it became subsumed by western influences.

When her first husband was accepted into the MBA program at Harvard, she tried to get a job as a journalist in Boston. She was hired by a professor at Harvard who believed it was easier to train a journalist to write about business than it would be to train an MBA student to write. After writing cases for the business school for two years she went through the program herself.

With her MBA and her Chinese language facility, Diane was recruited by management consultant McKinsey & Company, which was planning to run their Southeast Asian practice from Australia.

Primed by a video documentary on Australia which featured a man in khaki shorts and socks walking a wallaby on a leash, she arrived in 1979. At McKinsey she assisted clients in a variety of industries on strategic and organisational issues. Globally, Diane was a leader of McKinsey's organisation development and change management practice. In Australia, she led the firm's consumer goods and retailing practice.

Now a professional non-executive company director and management consultant, Diane is currently a director of Lend Lease Corporation, Woolworths Limited and Wattyl Limited. At Lend Lease she is Chairman of the Australian and Asian Property Services Group, which also includes Lend Lease Global Project Management, Civil and Civic and Lend Lease Development. She is also a trustee of the Sydney Opera House, a director of the Australian Institute of Management and a member of the Ascham School Council.

Akira Isogawa

Akira Isogawa was born in 1964 in Kyoto, Japan. He began designing garments after emigrating to Sydney in 1986 where he studied garment construction at the Sydney Institute of Technology. His first designs were sold in Sydney boutiques until 1993, when the Akira boutique opened in the Sydney suburb of Woollahra.

The first Isogawa parade – from the autumn/winter collection, *Not Made In Japan* – was unveiled at Sydney's Hogarth Gallery in 1994. It was a laneway parade which showcased Isogawa's Butoh-inspired deconstructed garments, handpainted and modelled by figures shrouded in black organza. The second Isogawa collection combined antique kimonos, brocade and embroidery reworked into new garments. His spring/summer 1996–1997 collection premiered at the inaugural Mercedes Australian Fashion Week in 1996. His multiple layering technique was a watershed in Australian chic and Isogawa was awarded the Australian Fashion Industry Awards' First Cut Award the same year. During 1997, Isogawa exhibited at the Powerhouse Museum's Fashion of the Year retrospective. It was followed by *Sartori*, his spring/summer 1997–1998 collection, and then *Botanica* the following season. Critics hailed *Botanica* as evidence of a new maturity in Australian fashion. The collection was acclaimed by leading media, including the *New York Times*, and was purchased by international stores, including Barney's New York.

In 1998 Isogawa was selected to exhibit in the Seppelt Contemporary Art Award at the Museum of Contemporary Art in Sydney. In collaboration with choreographer Graham Murphy, Isogawa also designed the costumes for the Sydney Dance Company's production of *Salome*.

Isogawa's garments are now sold throughout Australia and in London, Milan, Paris, New York, Japan, Hong Kong, Boston, Chicago, Santa Monica, Berlin, Munich, Singapore and New Zealand.

Chapter Three

Home-
sickness

Popular theories about acknowledging and expressing homesickness have changed over the last 30 years. No longer are people exhorted to smarten themselves up and think how lucky they are to be here. Rather, we allow and often encourage immigrants to grieve for those parts of their lives remembered and missed.

In any event, homesickness is part of the immigrant process, and is usually felt most strongly in the first two years. In many cases it is the women in the relationship who grieve for their families and the domestic customs they leave behind. These established patterns were part of the daily fabric of family life, and their absence is sorely felt.

Homesickness has another dimension which troubled some. How could you long for a place which had betrayed and abused you? Would it be different if you returned later, and was it disloyal to your new country to feel this grief?

Those who came alone and with a strong sense of adventure rarely suffered. They had left the old behind and were intent on succeeding in their new life. Somewhere on the journey they had crossed the threshold of the new life and could engage completely when they arrived. Many formed new families within the first two years, a powerful force for integrating into Australian life.

Homesickness could often be a positive influence. It helped keep the respect and practice of many customs and traditions of family life. For some families it became a challenge to remember and transfer the best aspects of their old lives to Australia. Many Italian families did this well.

The best cure for homesickness was to return to the place abandoned. So often it was realised that home was now Australia and the first home could be finally farewelled.

Elsa Atkin

I wasn't homesick for Bagdad – I hated living there – but I missed my friends. I had lots of friends because the European communities mixed a lot. We had the English Club and all that sort of thing, where everyone went and swam in the pool. We had friends from across the board. We had a big diplomatic corps and we had all the kids from those areas. We were exposed to huge and diverse cultural differences.

Caroline Baum

Oh the first two years it was very difficult to get out of bed. I mean I was acutely depressed. I had no money of my own. I had never been in a situation where I wasn't earning my own money; I had no job initially. Above all I had no support structure, so I not only had no family but I had no friends. The things I missed most acutely, and found most difficult to make, were friends.

Wolf Blass

Social life. I found it very hard socially to accept the isolation of life in a closed community like the Barossa Valley; to make contacts, in particular, with females, was very hard, coming from Paris, coming from London, coming from Frankfurt. There was early closing time. When you went to a dance you had to walk 200 metres to get a beer out of your FX Holden. The girls were sitting on the left-hand side, the boys on the right-hand side.

Arlene Chai

I went through a two-year depression when I first came. I would wake up in the middle of the night, I would cry, and I was so scared that my mother would hear. And you know what, she said 'I wept too'. There's an incredible grieving process, it's like you don't understand it; you think you've given up a lot but you don't give it up, it's always there. You don't walk away from things. But I think that's typical of separation; it makes you think you've lost something. That half full, half empty thing. You don't see that you are actually enriching yourself because it's a new experience. That does not come to you until years down the line. It's a grieving process.

Judy Cassab

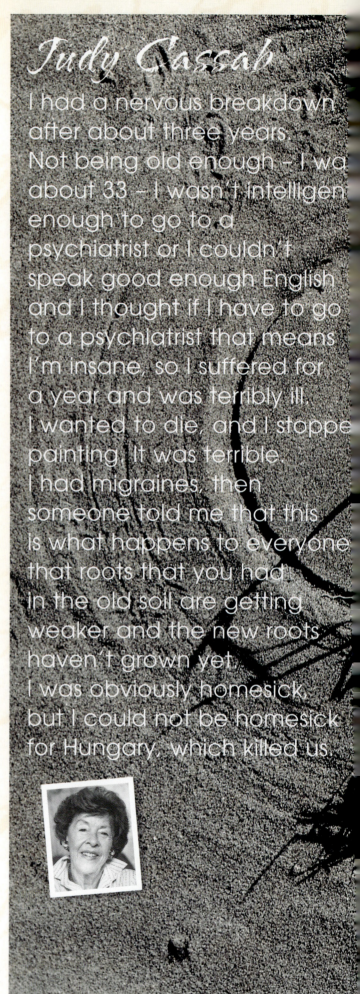

I had a nervous breakdown after about three years. Not being old enough – I was about 33 – I wasn't intelligent enough to go to a psychiatrist or I couldn't speak good enough English and I thought if I have to go to a psychiatrist that means I'm insane, so I suffered for a year and was terribly ill. I wanted to die, and I stopped painting. It was terrible. I had migraines, then someone told me that this is what happens to everyone that roots that you had in the old soil are getting weaker and the new roots haven't grown yet. I was obviously homesick, but I could not be homesick for Hungary, which killed us.

Josef Chromy

Christmas was very strange. I had always had white Christmases, with snow, and for a couple of years I had nice weather in Australia and I enjoyed it then. I always enjoyed being here and I set my mind to it to work hard and get somewhere.

Lou Klepac

Australia for me was interesting, but for my mother and father, when they arrived here, that was the end of their life. My father stopped the clock and that was it. He lived here more than he lived in Europe but nothing he did in Australia counted for anything. My mother's life was a misery. My mother became housebound, wouldn't go out of the house. She became agoraphobic, she wouldn't go out.

Vivi Germanos-Koutsounadis

Well, they never spoke about their homesickness, but yes, they were homesick. They told us stories. That was really great, because that maintained our contact with our families. Because I was very conscientious, I was the correspondent. I would write all the letters back and forth from home.

Petro Georgiou

I think my mother was quite genuinely homesick. She had a well-established family and I think she had to substantially adjust. She is fine now. If you put my mother on a jet that was hijacked by Arab terrorists she would be the first one they let off. A very strong lady.

Sir James Gobbo

Italians always suffer from homesickness, I think. Unlike other people, they have a real sense of affection for the region they lived in. It is not a nationalistic thing at all, it is tied to the relatives, it is tied to a place, the particular part of Italy they come from. You don't find that with some other countries.

Bill Jegorow

Time changes perceptions. I have been back to Germany quite a few times, particularly the little town where I spent about seven years during and after the war, and I still have some friends there. I had some pleasant experiences too, so I can't say that everything was absolutely bad. But by and large, Australia is very much home.

Akira Isogawa

Maybe the first year, or second year, occasionally. It is not depressing every single day, but occasionally I was homesick, especially with the language barrier. I guess I am busy here in Sydney and enjoying this sort of life.

George Lapaine

At first no, because there was a great excitement, everything was new. After a while I got terribly homesick. I had a girlfriend before I left Italy and out here it was impossible to communicate with Aussie girls because of one, the language and two, there was a hell of a lot of prejudice in those days against these strange foreigners with their fancy clothes, moccasin shoes and different cut of clothing, so it was terribly difficult.

56 | A Fair Go – Portraits of the Australian Dream

Anita Mak

There were times in the past when I missed family and friends, ways of doing things, aspects of the lifestyle. I was brought up in a metropolitan lifestyle, but then I have been able to catch up with aspects of that by occasional travel to Hong Kong and also other parts of the world.

Rolando Ramos

I miss the mountains. That is something I miss still. When we arrived there was the space, but sometimes there was a flatness. There weren't mountains, for instance. Chile is surrounded by mountains and there isn't far you have to walk to see a big range of mountains, quite high, with snow. I miss that. It was very easy to get orientation in Chile because you can see this is north or south because the mountains were there. It was a geographical signpost, but here there is none. So that is something I miss in terms of the country.

Juliana Nkrumah

Somebody said to me last week, 'You are different. You have changed.' I said, 'One ought to change in life in order to continue on.' If I get stuck in my culture I won't be able to be the person I have chosen to be, an Australian. That is one thing that has happened to me. On the other hand, in my life as an African, I suppose what I miss is the family structure. The ability to be in my place amongst the huge extended family. To take my place there and be a woman of Africa, to be a Ghanaian woman.

Gladys Roach

No. I was pregnant straight away and my son Vijay was born in Adelaide. We somehow managed. The challenge was not to let them know in India that there were hard times. So I sent home photographs standing in front of other people's cars and houses. They thought anyone who lived in a foreign country was supposedly well-off, so I sent these photographs home and tried not to write about how difficult life was.

Neville Roach

Well, I missed the food, my family, my mother, my father as well, but particularly my mother and Gladys. In terms of day-to-day living, food. It was just an absolute impossibility to get spiced food anywhere. Food was very ordinary in Australia in the early 1960s. The Chinese restaurants were the old ones where people had stopped cooking real Chinese food. I would go to eat there but it was terrible.

Miguel Sanz

I missed a lifestyle. I missed my grandparents. The way that we lived, all my family was around us. I had an aunt and an uncle who went to France prior to us coming to Australia, but apart from them the whole family structure was there. My grandparents were there. I guess I was spoilt. I loved Spain, I loved the food. The family structure that we had there, we didn't have here. Here we didn't have my uncles, we didn't have my grandfather. I had no-one that I could run to. I found it hard in that respect.

Joe Saragossi

Actually, conversation. The level of sophistication on world politics or local politics was something I missed. Also the sporting events were different. In those days they didn't televise or broadcast the baseball results from America, so you lost track of all the things you did keep track of.

Dagmar Schmidmaier

The family was split between Germany and Palestine. I think my mother missed that very strong sense of community that they had there, and I suppose a lifestyle they had built up. I think she really enjoyed the different cultures as well. Palestine in those days was a very multicultural environment. She was very used to that and she enjoyed travel, but she was very happy here. She loved Sydney; she loved the ocean.

Jim Trambas

I was sick but not homesick in a way because we came by ourselves. My friend went to Melbourne and I went to Sydney. I was walking in Parramatta one Saturday morning and there were thousands of heads I could see walking up and down the street shopping, and I felt so strange I didn't have anybody. That day I felt very, very lonely. I think that is the only day I felt like that. Eventually you make friends.

Kostya Tszyu

I was very homesick. My wife cried for over a year every day, every night. Me, I was busy. When you are busy there is no time to miss anything.

In the beginning it was friends and family, but now family is here and friends have been here for a visit, some of the relatives as well. For me to go back there is difficult now.

Ilija Kovacevic

I miss my friends and the life I had in Bosnia because I had a good job and I was settled down with a house and a car and I had good wages. We went often to the soccer. I had lots of friends who sometimes stayed overnight. No more. When I came here I thought about that life, things like 'is anybody thinking about me?' And I think about my life there and my house and I wonder who has been killed, who is still alive.

Agnes Whiten

For two years I carried my passport in my bag of jewellery. I was terribly homesick and I was ready to go any time. The first time I fought with my husband it was because of homesickness. I had no maid, I had to do everything, which was a shock. I come from a middle-class family and being a professional, I mean, you don't do these things back home. It was a cultural shock. Of course I lived in Manila, which is a very cosmopolitan city, and Brisbane, then, at 5.30pm was dead. Can you imagine in 1972 everything was dead? Manila never sleeps.

Mala Dharmananda

I was homesick. I wanted to go back to India and go to boarding school soon after we arrived here. We came at the end of the year. Because there were five of us, my mother put some of us into school to make it easier. It was November and there were only a couple of weeks of school left. I hadn't been to a mixed school at all. I couldn't understand them and, I dare say, they couldn't understand me. I didn't understand what they ate; I wanted to have rice at lunchtime, not sandwiches. We'd never had sandwiches like that. I came back from two weeks at school and said 'I don't like it here; I want to go back home.'

Ted Johnson

My mother was more homesick than anyone else. She certainly suffered because she came from a big family, as did my father. It is a pretty commonplace thing, but those of us who had to go to work, or school, or whatever, had an immediate reference point for social contact. But my mother was the one who didn't feel as acclimatised or as comfortable as we would have liked her to be. It wasn't a time when, if you came and didn't like it, you could go back. You made a commitment. We made a decision to come and we came, so she had this sense of inevitability that she may not return, and that's a pretty testing thing for people.

George Mure

I had a very privileged life in Kenya. It sounds awful in this politically correct time, but I played polo for school sport. Took my own polo pony to school with me, so it was a very privileged life. My stepfather was a doctor in Kenya, a specialist.

Chapter Three – Homesickness | 61

Wadim (Bill) Jegorow AM MBE

A poster in a West German refugee camp, which proclaimed Australia as the Land of Tomorrow, was temptation enough for his family, refugees from Poland who had fled Russia after the revolution. Bill was 16 at the time and, recognising that Australia was a country of egalitarianism and a fair go, he helped make the decision to choose Australia over the United States or Canada. When they arrived at Bonegilla in June of 1951 it was bitterly cold and, one refugee camp being pretty much like another, not much different from the camps they had left in Germany.

Bill's older sister was already living with her husband in Woy Woy, so the family headed for Pearl Beach, an area they found utterly inspiring. Despite having learned English in Germany, the spoken word just rolled right over the top of Bill's head for his first six months in Australia. Then, suddenly, he could understand what was said and from then felt at home. He actually considered Australia to be his country right from the beginning.

When Bill finished high school he won a cadetship with the Child Welfare Department allowing him to study Arts and Social Studies and take on a role as a child welfare worker. He was one of very few men involved in that field at the time. He became a parole officer in the NSW Prisons Department in 1958 and, after admission as a Barrister, practised in Sydney from 1965–1970. He rejoined the NSW Public Service as a lawyer and became full-time Deputy Chairman of the Ethnic Affairs Commission in 1980.

Within two years Bill was naturalised and joined the Sydney University Regiment and the Labor Party almost at the same time. 'I was a pretty committed socialist for a period of two years after I joined the Party,' he says, 'before I came to realise there are no simple solutions to humanity's problems. Socialism is certainly not, in itself, a solution.'

Having an accent, knowing the problems of adjustment and wanting to help, Bill eventually became foundation chairperson of the Ethnic Communities' Council of New South Wales and the Federation of Ethnic Communities' Councils of Australia. The Ethnic Communities' Council successfully lobbied the Wran State Government to establish the Ethnic Affairs Commission of New South Wales, the first such body in Australia, in 1976.

As alderman of Ashfield Council from 1959–1987, Bill was deeply involved in community welfare and development work. He was a member of the multicultural advisory bodies to the Malcolm Fraser and Bob Hawke Federal governments and he has continued his involvement with the Ethnic Communities' Council and with local government.

Ted Johnson

Ted Johnson's father did some thorough research of countries the family might migrate to, visiting Canada ('too cold'), the United States ('too many Irish already') and South Africa ('trouble brewing') before settling on Australia. Part of the Irish diaspora which left Ireland in the 1950s and 1960s, the Johnson family sold a guest house in Dublin and a pub at Balls Bridge, and arrived in Adelaide complete with furniture and car, ready to start all over again. The family soon moved to Melbourne, where Ted's father had a job lined up as a catering manager.

A 25-year career as a banker saw Ted rise through the ranks at the ANZ Bank before becoming managing director of the Bank of South Australia, a position he held for four years until the bank was sold to Advance Bank. In 1995 he was appointed managing director and chief executive officer of the Royal Automobile Club of Victoria.

The family had become Australian citizens once they started to travel; Ted became a citizen when he did his national service in 1958. While he was an Australian citizen, he still travelled on his Irish passport until the rules changed in the early 1980s and he needed an Australian passport for re-entry into the country. However, the real turning point, the point at which he knew he had definitely become an Australian, happened in 1992 when Ireland played Australia in the World Cup finals at Landsdowne Road.

'I was watching it on the television and when the Irish scored a try in the last two minutes and took the lead, I thought: "Shit, I hope they don't win," he says. 'When Australia replied with a try, I was euphoric.'

Ted values Australia because 'It's not a life that's predetermined by birth, by religion. I think we're tolerant; I think we grab onto everything that's new, sometimes too fiercely. That shows a sense of immaturity, but that's good; I like that. We're trying to seek ways of being a better community, a better society. That's what I like about it.'

Elena Kats-Chernin

Elena Kats-Chernin was born in Russia and began her musical studies at Yaroslavl Music School. After matriculating at the age of 14 she proceeded with her musicological studies at the Gnesina Musical College in Moscow. In 1975 she emigrated with her family to Australia and entered the diploma course at the NSW State Conservatorium of Music.

She says she played no part in the decision to come to Australia. It was her father who, refused permission to visit his sister who lived here, decided that it was a good time for the whole family to join her permanently.

While still a student, Elena received numerous awards and scholarships, two of which took her to further study in Germany.

She stayed in Europe for over a decade but made several trips back to Australia for performances of her work. She wrote for the theatre and composed several ballets and much incidental music for the state theatres in Vienna, Berlin, Hamburg and Bochum. She collaborated as a performer with the German choreographer Reinhild Hoffman in experimental theatre productions in Tokyo, Lisbon and Karlsruhe. Elena returned to Australia in 1994 and now lives in Sydney.

She was represented at the 1994 Munchener Biennale with her piece for two pianists and a dancer, *Coco's Last Collection*. Her orchestral works, *Stairs*, *Transfer* and *Retonica*, have all been performed by ABC orchestras. Her piece *Clocks* (1993) was premiered by Ensemble Modern and has had numerous performances, the most recent being by the Juilliard Ensemble in New York in 1998.

During the last two years, Elena's Portrait CD *Clocks*, performed by the Sydney Alpha Ensemble, has been released by ABC Classics. Her two operas, *Iphis* and *Matricide*, have received very successful premiere seasons. Her most recent success was the premiere of a major project, the composition of a score for the silent movie *Abwege*, which was a huge success in Germany and then in Paris.

'I would do it all over again,' she says. 'I would like to have been born here. I think I missed out on having my school years in Australia; the later you come, the harder it is to make friends here. I would like to know more about childhood here. I feel so privileged that I can be here. The thought never leaves me. I hope it doesn't sound corny, but it's really true. I'm so happy in this environment and I feel so grateful that I've got this place and I've got my space where I can work and I've got my little piano, even if it's broken. There are a lot of things I feel pleased about, even if they're not perfect. Nothing in my life is perfect, and I don't like writing perfect music. I like things to be slightly on edge and slightly not right, and it's the same with Australia. It's not perfect, but it's great.'

Lou Klepac OAM

Lou Klepac was born in the former Yugoslavia and developed his interest in art in Venice, where he lived as a child and first went to school. He emigrated to Australia in 1950 and was educated at the University of Western Australia, where he was the art critic for the student newspaper, *The Pelican*.

From 1958 to 1964 he lived in Europe, where he became familiar with all the great art collections. He returned to Perth in 1964 and became the Curator of Paintings at the Art Gallery of Western Australia. He then became Curator of Paintings at the Art Gallery of South Australia, and also lectured in the School of Architecture at the University of Adelaide. He was also the art critic for the Adelaide *News*.

After five years in London, from 1970 to 1974, he returned to Perth and was Senior Curator and then Deputy Director of the Art Gallery of Western Australia.

He has organised many exhibitions, including Sickert Paintings (1968); Contemporary Drawing (1977); Contemporary Australian Drawing (1978); Sickert Drawings (1979); the Drawings of Russell Drysdale (1980); Russell Drysdale Paintings (1985) and Giorgio Morandi Paintings and Etchings (1997). He is the author of several books, including *Horace Trenerry* (1970); *Russell Drysdale, Life and Work* (1983); *James Gleeson, Landscape Out Of Nature* (1987); and *Judy Cassab, Portraits of Artists and Friends* (1998).

He was a founding member of the Australian Art Galleries Association, a member of AICA for 25 years and has been President of the Frederick May Foundation for Italian Studies at Sydney University. He has been a member of the Advisory Committee of the National Trust of Australia's S.H. Ervin Gallery since 1984, and in 1980 he was appointed Cavaliere della Repubblica Italiana for his services to Italian art. He was awarded an OAM in 1996.

Since 1980 Lou Klepac has lived in Sydney, where he has established The Beagle Press, which is devoted exclusively to publishing books on fine art.

Judit Korner

Escaping from the revolution in Hungary in 1956, Judit Korner and her mother, an industrial chemist, arrived in Australia in 1957 after a short stay in Austria. Judit clearly remembers the drama and excitement of escaping on a train, walking through paddocks in the snow and covering her back with a sheet so that she wouldn't be seen. In Austria, Judit and her mother, Suzanna, were cared for by nuns in a convent boarding school. With her mother working, Judit was free to wander the streets of Vienna marvelling at shops which sold bananas and oranges, things she had never seen in Budapest. Given the choice of emigrating to Sweden, Italy, America or Australia, they eventually chose Australia because it was so far from Russia. After leaving Vienna they spent some time in an army camp in Salzburg before being taken on an old US troop carrier, supplied by the United Nations, across the French and Italian Riviera, ending up first in Sydney and finally in Hobart. Judit remembers the ship coming to Australia was full of refugees, women who had nothing, who did not know where they were going and did not speak the new language, yet still managed to have facials.

'They didn't have two cents to bless themselves with,' she says. 'The clothes we wore were from assorted charitable institutes, and if you were really lucky you had good shoes; if you weren't, you didn't. It was a situation of a mismatched bunch of people, from scientists to linguists to opera singers to labourers – and all the women were having facials with butter, eggs and honey that the American sailors had in abundance. They were in a situation where they didn't know whether they would be alive tomorrow, yet they wanted silk stockings, they wanted lipstick, they wanted perfume, they wanted face creams. It just didn't make sense.'

Judit paid her way through school in Hobart by working in a pharmacy, where she soon became fascinated by the prettiness of the lipsticks and the perfumes and considered that if she were to go to Sydney for her university studies it might help her finances if she could also learn how to do beauty treatments. She arrived in Sydney to study dentistry, missed the enrolment date and studied dental mechanics instead. She then found that being a female dental mechanic meant being unemployable, so she fell back on the beauty treatments, and the rest is history. There are five Madame Korner Salons throughout Australia and Judit considers her greatest contribution to be increasing awareness of the terrible damage the Australian sun does to Australian skin.

Chapter Four
Citizenship

This year Australia celebrates 50 years of Citizenship. Citizenship is about loyalty to Australia and its people, a shared belief in the democratic process, respect for the rights and liberties of other Australians and a commitment to uphold and obey Australian laws.

Becoming a citizen is seen as a symbol of commitment to Australia, and immigrants are officially encouraged to take this step. Citizenship ceremonies are significant rites of passage, well remembered by the families. It is often the moment when people begin to identify themselves as Australian.

The Nationality and Citizenship Act of 1948 required a five-year wait for naturalisation, although many of the people interviewed recalled a shorter waiting period. In 1973 the waiting period was reduced to three years, and by 1984 it had been reduced to two years, making it one of the shortest qualification periods in the world. It is surely ironic that many immigrants arriving post-1949 became citizens before our own Indigenous people, who did not gain this right until 1967.

The policy of making immigrants into citizens is a powerful success factor in our immigration program, and encourages civic responsibility while guaranteeing equality before the law.

The take-up rate of Citizenship varies, with New Zealanders having the lowest rate: only 50 per cent of those resident for 20 years have become citizens. By comparison, those of non-English speaking background (NESB) had a take-up rate of over 80 per cent. This reflects a general pattern relating to country of origin, and one could argue that the NESB rate indicates a much higher commitment to Australia from these people than those from English speaking backgrounds (ESB). Often immigrants from New Zealand and the United Kingdom see themselves as different, and not in need of Citizenship as they are British subjects.

When I approached some people from those countries for interviews they were surprised to be categorised in this way.

Embracing Citizenship is a positive action, but if one has to give up other Citizenship it can cause conflict within families. For some, this is the last link with the past, and breaking it is painful. Becoming a parent makes a difference, as children born to legal immigrants are automatically Australian citizens. This is often an incentive for the parents to become naturalised.

Elsa Atkin

When I got married in 1966 we went overseas and when I came back I felt I was really, really an Australian person. When I was overseas I realised how Australian I was. My affinity was with Australia and Australian values, and it was so strong that it really was brought into relief when I was overseas. When I came back, that was it. Of course, once you have children, that's really it.

Paul Boyatzis

We came to Australia because we wanted to come to Australia because it was a better place, and we came here to stay. Therefore, from that moment, one becomes Australian in the sense that you are leaving a place where you no longer want to be and you are moving to another country. Not on a temporary basis, to work for five years and collect money and then go back. We came here to stay. Therefore, we moved to Australia to become Australians. That was the mood of the time and it still is.

Caroline Baum

I think of myself as an Australian, but I also think of myself as a European. I haven't had to give anything up. I haven't had to surrender a passport. If I had to surrender a passport, I might not have done it. I went through a French education system and I am very used to my European roots. I am very committed to them.

Arlene Chai

In 1990 my sister and I went to Europe and then to Manila to see my grandparents, and I can remember feeling that I didn't quite belong. My sister's boyfriend picked us up from the airport when we arrived back in Sydney and we were driving across the Harbour Bridge and it was the most joyous feeling – I had my head out the window and I said, 'I'm home, I'm home'.

Mala Dharmananda

I think when I went to university I called myself an Australian. But I think of myself now as an Indian Australian. It's when you go away that you make a statement about where you're from. When you go back to India no-one asks you where you come from; they assume you migrated for whatever reason but you are still Indian. Even now when I go back to India, I still belong in India. I may live somewhere else but I'm still part of India. It's when you go to other countries that you say 'I come from Australia.' I'm proud of being Australian, and I get irritated when they make criticisms of Australia, except for the cricket.

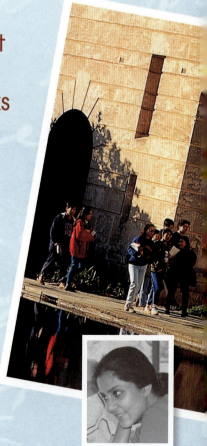

72 | A Fair Go – Portraits of the Australian Dream

Josef Chromy

I felt Australian before I was naturalised because I could see so much freedom. I could start a business. I could go and speak to the bank whether I was Australian or not. I could buy a house and I could get a loan whether or not I was naturalised. So I felt Australian before I was naturalised.

Anita Donaldson

I feel more Australian than not, but there are times when I'm very conscious of my background. I've gone back to where I was born. It was an interesting experience actually being there, even though I had no memory of the place. It underlined for me that I am, at heart, very much a European. A very simple thinker. I don't like Australian native trees. I don't actually like the harsh sun. I can only attribute that to something European. It's intuitive, it's deeply rooted, but I sense myself ultimately as European. But it hasn't persuaded me to go and live in Europe, because I have family here. My family made the journey because they had to; they had no choice. It's easy for people of that generation to idealise what they had. My mother was saying 'Oh, fifty years in this country'. And the reality is that she only spent 24 years in Latvia and yet she had this picture of Latvia which I suspect is a little bit ideal, and she's always wanting to go back.

Vivi Germanos-Koutsounadis

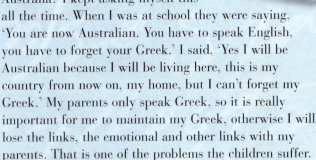

I had to become naturalised when I became 16. The thing is, what is Australia? I kept asking myself this all the time. When I was at school they were saying, 'You are now Australian. You have to speak English, you have to forget your Greek.' I said, 'Yes I will be Australian because I will be living here, this is my country from now on, my home, but I can't forget my Greek.' My parents only speak Greek, so it is really important for me to maintain my Greek, otherwise I will lose the links, the emotional and other links with my parents. That is one of the problems the children suffer.

Sir James Gobbo

I thought of myself as an Australian from the very beginning when I went to school. I knew I was born in Australia. I think, like anybody, any immigrant to Australia who is of school age, the pressure for conformity is overwhelming. I think that schools are very conformist. That can be a very good thing but it exerts enormous pressure. I wanted to be accepted more than anything in the world; I wanted to be Australian.

Diane Grady

I guess it just became clear that we were never going to return to the United States. Our kids were totally Australian. My husband is American and he's been here 30 years. I guess it just became so apparent that Australia was home so it was silly not to. He did it before I did – to be honest I couldn't do it while I had to swear allegiance to the Queen. He actually swore allegiance to the Queen, and I sat there and watched him and I just thought, 'No, I can't do this'.

Elena Kats-Chernin

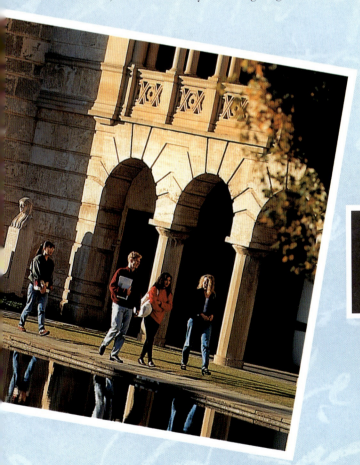

Two or three years after we arrived we became Australian citizens. It made us feel proud and you do feel you have achieved something. We waited for it so long. I already felt Australian by that time. I was integrated. Every time I moved somewhere, be it Europe or back here after Russia, it takes about two years every time to actually feel totally at home.

Les Cassar

The moment I started working for Qantas I started thinking of myself as Australian. Qantas was an Australian icon – it still is – and it was a government company. When I went out representing them I was very proud.

Lou Klepac

What happened was, when I was given a Bible to kiss to become an Australian citizen, they said I had to make an allegiance to the Queen. Everyone talked about England, you see. I was doing English at university. Everyone said 'home, home, home'. In Western Australia, more than anywhere else, England was much more important, because it was the mother country. So, having sort of steeped myself in English culture, literature, I was English, already, from the inside. The Croatians always looked to London as their home; the Serbs always looked to Paris as their home.

George Lapaine

That's a hard one. It is a bit hard because when you are living in a society you can consider yourself all sorts of things, but if the people around you don't consider you as an Australian, in the traditional Anglo-Celtic sense, then it is very hard to impose your own belief that you are an Aussie on other people. I often wonder if people who are born overseas, and actually spend their formative years overseas, can actually call themselves anything else.

Ted Kunkel

I have two daughters. They were born in 1972 and 1975, and they were both born in Australia. So the decision was made very shortly after that to become an Aussie. I think it was around about that time also that Prime Minister Fraser, I think, was rattling the sabre and New Zealand was being made the scapegoat as the drug alley to Australia. They were talking about New Zealanders being made to carry passports to get in and out of Australia. My boss at the time said to me, 'Okay, Sunshine, you'd better become an Australian.' But it was the girls who really made us become Australians. Now the only time I don't think of myself as an Australian is when the All Blacks play. I do revert under those circumstances.

Dai Le

I thought, 'I am going back to Vietnam and I will see my country again, see my grandmother again,' and stuff like that, but then people looked at me in the street like I was an overseas Vietnamese, like a traitor, that I had gone away and made it with all this money and now was coming back and trying to bargain with them. Like 'how dare you bargain the price down; you know how hard our life is,' type of thing. Maybe it is just me, but the culture was totally strange to me. Two weeks there and I just couldn't wait to get back.

Tan Le

When I went to Vietnam recently there was certainly a link, a connection that wasn't there when I went to Hong Kong, Malaysia, Thailand or China. But in Vietnam I felt it. There was a bond that was more special than Asia. When we flew back to Melbourne I felt that we were really home, and I was so happy to be home. The familiar surroundings, the cars, the streets, it's all in order – a stable, safe society that I've become accustomed to. I recognise Vietnam as being my heritage, but it's not my home.

Nelson Leong

If nobody asks where I come from I feel 100 per cent Australian. When anybody asks me where I come from, automatically I switch back to East Timor. I am so comfortable in this country and I have lots of friends who have never discriminated against me. I am part of their society. I mix well, so I feel 100 per cent Australian even though when I look in the mirror I am different. My heart is here in this country. I am so comfortable with the people, the lifestyle, the environment.

Anita Mak

I became an Australian in 1987. It was a significant ceremony on Australia Day in the National Library. We had to sing the National Anthem. We didn't have trees to take away but I still kept the words to the National Anthem and put my Citizenship Certificate in a safe place. I think it's a very important passage. It shows an identity. I have a number of identities; being an Australian is an important identity, but it's not my sole identity. It's my priority identity. In terms of cultural identity, the fact that I am Chinese is very high up, and being born and raised in Hong Kong is also an important part of my identity. Being a psychologist, being a researcher, being a woman, being a mother and so on. I have a whole range of identities.

George Mure

It was in the Whitlam years when I became naturalised. I just went along and swore allegiance to the Queen, I think, which seemed pretty silly since I was a Pom anyway. But I wanted to be Australian because I wasn't really English, because I had been brought up in Kenya, and I didn't think of myself as African either. I felt Australian, I would say certainly, from 1962 onwards. I have never considered myself anything else.

Judit Korner

I became an Australian a long, long time ago. They didn't make too much fanfare at the time, but now they have fandangos on Australia Day, which I think is really nice. I was stateless, I was a refugee, so I had to become something. So it was not a question of 'I shall give up my Citizenship'. Now I believe I can have a Hungarian passport. I've been daydreaming about that. But an Australian passport works really well for me.

Satendra Nandan

I became an Australian citizen, in fact I rejected Fijian nationality, once the current regime was in power. Once my passport ran out I became an Australian citizen. The Citizenship ceremony implies this huge commitment and advantages and other things. It was not so much that I love being an Australian citizen, because I knew so little about Australia; it was more a rejection of something to which I was born.

Juliana Nkrumah

I didn't become an Australian citizen for convenience. I became an Australian citizen to give back to Australia what it has given me – my protection. As a result of that I need to contribute to this land. If that means giving up some of the things of my own land, then I might do that.

Sir Arvi Parbo

I suppose I never really thought about it in a conscious sense. I was naturalised in 1954, I think. This was before I completed the university course. We just had the refugee papers. This is where I came to establish myself and my new life. I never thought of myself as anything else. I came here to stay.

Rolando Ramos

In many ways I never felt comfortable in Chile. There were many things that Chile couldn't give me in terms of my own aspirations. I travelled to Brazil a couple of times as well, when I was in South America, and I never felt quite comfortable travelling. So when I got here, I felt this was it. I felt quite free travelling. Not necessarily feeling 'I am this from this part'. I like to see myself with the freedom to be able to travel, to move, for instance. So the moment I reached Australia I felt like I belonged to this country.

Gladys Roach

There was not much incentive to become Australian citizens because when we came out, if you were members of the Commonwealth, you could vote, so we had all the rights and duties of citizens without actually having to change our Citizenship. Also, it was required that we give up our Indian Citizenship to become Australian. India requires it. We didn't want to do that, so that was what held us back. But more than that it was an emotional commitment, I guess, to India. When we did decide to become Australian citizens, I felt, for me anyway, that I knew at that time that I definitely would not live anywhere else in the world. I wanted to live in Australia.

Fred Shahin

When I got back here after my first overseas trip in 1987, I felt I was coming home. The rest of the time I had criticised the system. I did not understand how, in Adelaide, they had a cemetery for dogs and people. Overseas they cremate them because there's no space, but when I got back after that trip I started talking about how they respect life, human beings here, how they treat elderly people here. There is no poverty in Australia, unlike overseas. Overseas your biggest worry is how to secure education for your children, and that's very expensive.

Neville Roach

If you had to barrack for Australia in cricket, I think there would be many fewer citizens here. If that was part of the Citizenship pledge – that I will no longer support India and now support Australia – then most Indian-Australians probably wouldn't have become citizens. Again multiculturalism, it's just a minor area, but it is an example of where you can have affection and links to your previous country while feeling at home and comfortable here.

Jim Trambas

I was very fortunate because I felt very Australian the day I came here. I said, 'When in Rome do as the Romans do.' Naturally I felt very proud. When I was working in Canberra, we stayed on the fourth floor of the Canberra Hotel and they said to us, 'President Lyndon Johnson will be arriving in Canberra and we want you to move to the top floor.' I thought to myself, 'Gee, if I was in Greece, a worker working for a company, and a prime minister came to stay in the hotel, I wouldn't have a chance to be within five hundred metres of it, and I am staying in the same hotel.'

Kostya Tszyu

Sometimes I feel I am more Australian than someone who was born here. The reason is that I am trying to do a lot for this country. The people sometimes who are born here are not doing anything for the country. I am proud to call myself 'Aussie', and when I go anywhere I try to explain to people about Australia, because everyone just thinks of the kangaroo, the same thing I thought about it. I love this country.

Agnes Whiten

The thing that cured me was, you go back after two years, the friends and your family have moved on. Even now, after 27 years, what you look back to was the very first time you left. The very first time when the plane left I was crying; I was leaving my country, and I was singing my national anthem inside. But every time I have gone back since, it is different. Bill says, 'I can't understand you. When we are in Manila you want to go back to Brisbane. When we are in Brisbane you want to go back to Manila.' The only thing that really cured me was after 14 years I became naturalised because I had the children. I knew then, when I had the children, I was not going back.

Wilson Wu

In 1989 we became citizens. It was a proud moment. Good citizens are what we want to be.

Chapter Four – Citizenship | 77

Ilija Kovacevic

The 1992 war in Yugoslavia forced Bosnian-born Ilija Kovacevic to flee to Germany. A civil engineer, he had been employed as a project manager building roads and bridges before the war started and fire destroyed his home and the company he worked for. He stayed as a refugee in Germany for 16 months, realised it was only a temporary solution and he and his brother applied for Australian visas. He arrived in 1994, found a part-time job as a cleaner and caretaker for the Yass Shire Council and took English classes on the side. His part-time job became permanent and he has since enrolled in a civil engineering course in Canberra. His wife, a chemical engineer, works three jobs – as a housemaid cleaning hotel rooms, picking tomatoes and cooking at a relative's hotel. Although it was a tough decision at first, Ilija knows that emigrating was the right decision, particularly for his two children, whose future he worried about. 'Their life as they grow up will be different to mine,' he says. 'They don't know about how I was living in Bosnia. I'm still OK, if I finish my school, if I can get a better job. If not, it's not important. I'm still OK, healthy. I can, during the next 10 years or so, I can build houses and I can get my own house without borrowing money from the bank. I'd like to spend more time to help my children because I don't have anything special in my life that I need to get or reach.'

On multiculturalism he says: 'Sometimes we go to Canberra and there are lots of Croatian poeple there and they spend lots of time talking about what happened there. People are still talking against the other side. They spend more time talking about that than what's happening here, I think. What's happening in Bosnia is more important to them than what is happening here. People still live in ethnic groups.'

In 1997 Ilija won a special award presented by the Rotary Club of Yass in honour of his high standards, commitment, care and personal pride in his workmanship in the field of services as a caretaker. He has also achieved certificates for computing skills for the office.

Ted Kunkel

In 1968 when Ted Kunkel realised the opportunities for graduates in New Zealand were limited to the world of agriculture, he headed for Australia to work in secondary industry, where the opportunities and the money were much more attractive. Armed with a Bachelor of Science and a double major in chemistry and zoology, and with a year's experience in the New Zealand wine industry, he wanted to get into production management. Carlton United Breweries had advertised for assistant brewers and he was accepted.

From his start as an assistant brewer he rose up the chain and was appointed production manager of CUB's Fiji breweries. After three years in Suva he did a stint back in Australia in various production and general management roles, then in 1987 was sent to Canada to run Carling O'Keefe Breweries and then the Molson Breweries. In 1992 he was appointed president and chief executive officer of Foster's Brewing Group, which focuses on the beer, wine and leisure industries.

'I would like to think that I was the man that led the team that pulled Foster's back from the brink,' he says. 'We were technically broke in 1992; just about gone. Now it's resurrected as an Australian icon. You have to feel quite passionate about it. The other "Vegemites" have gone; the Arnotts have gone; even Qantas is 25 per cent owned by British Airways. Foster's has a broadly spread share register and is majority owned by Australians and we are very proud to have achieved that.'

As a New Zealander, he never considered himself a migrant, because there was never the trauma of immigration. 'In those early days you didn't need a passport between Australia and New Zealand,' he says. 'That immediately differentiated the New Zealand immigrant from virtually all the others. Australia almost considered New Zealand as the seventh, eighth and ninth states. The Kiwis thought the other way; Australia was the fourth, fifth, sixth, seventh, eighth, ninth. You never really considered yourself not entitled to be here.'

George Lapaine MBE

Born in Idria, a small town north of Trieste, George Lapaine arrived in Australia in 1951 at the age of 15. An only child whose father's timber business was destroyed during the war, George's family decided to leave that part of Italy, or Yugoslavia, as it had become.

Australia was chosen because there was work and a good climate. The recruitment posters showed space, sun and smiles. They dreamt of cane cutting in North Queensland, earning a lot of money and then moving to one of the cities.

The Lapaines had no English when they arrived at Bonegilla Migrant Hostel and, sadly, when the work in Queensland was handed out, the father had to refuse because his son was not considered a suitable work mate. Too small.

The Queensland dream over, they moved to Sydney and factory work, and the family was separated. George was placed in a railway camp at Leichhardt and went to work as a store boy for NSW Railways. He stayed for the required two years and, at 18, went back to school at Christian Brothers College in Waverley. This happened because his English teacher intervened and asked the school to take him. Despite his poor English and his isolation (there was only one other Italian-born kid at Waverley College), he got his Leaving Certificate. He won a scholarship to Sydney University, where he studied Arts for two years and then enrolled in Law and worked as an Articled Clerk.

In 1963 George was admitted as a solicitor of the Supreme Court of NSW. He set up a practice in Leichhardt immediately, and for nearly 30 years ran a successful practice whose clients were mainly Italians establishing businesses in real estate, construction, restaurants and travel. They needed professional help from someone who spoke Italian.

That role extended pro bono into the community, and George worked with Italian-based community organisations such as CO.AS.IT. This service was recognised by the Italian government's award of the Order of Cavaliere al Merito in 1973, and in 1982 he was awarded an MBE for services to migrants.

George Lapaine is currently a full-time instructor in Property and Commercial Law at the NSW College of Law and a frequent speaker on the legal responsibilities of interpreters.

Chapter Four – Citizenship | 81

Dai Le

In April 1975, in the chaos that surrounded the fall of Saigon, Dai Le, her mother and two younger sisters found themselves bundled into a Jeep, taken to a ship and subsequently dumped into a GI camp in the Philippines. Years later she found out that several of her relatives were supposed to accompany them that day but never made it to the ship. For four years the little family waited for their husband and father to arrive at the displaced people's camp in the Philippines to take them to America, where everyone else was headed. When it became obvious that he wasn't coming, Dai's mother decided they would join a second escape attempt, and after 10 days at sea they were picked up by a Hong Kong patrol boat and interned in a refugee camp for another year. Their application to go to America was eventually accepted, but at the last moment Dai's mother decided to turn it down. They would go, she said, 'to an island with good education and where there was no Vietnamese community, with no memories of the war and no memories of the country they came from, so they could start all over again'. They applied to, and were accepted by, Australia. They arrived in 1979 and were taken by bus to Wollongong, driving through national parks that the new arrivals feared were yet more jungles. Because there were so few Vietnamese in Wollongong at that time, Dai Le's family was forced to join the whole community right away, blending immediately with Australians of various backgrounds and having to speak English from the start.

After six months studying law at university, Dai dropped out, rebelling against the pressure placed on Asian students by their families and relishing the freedom Australia offered her not to be a doctor, not to be a lawyer. Now a journalist with the ABC Radio National's Social and History Unit, where she produces radio documentaries, Dai feels her greatest contribution will be to act as a bridge between the Vietnamese people and the wider Australian society, to tell the stories of Vietnamese like herself who escaped and whose stories have yet to be told.

'I would love to tell that story so that you could understand me a bit more and I can alleviate your fear about this increased number of Asians in Australia,' she says. 'I hope to increase people's awareness of how to deal with Vietnamese culture. Possibly by understanding the Vietnamese culture they can have a light understanding of other Asian cultures. We all have different experiences, but to be able to understand one Asian culture, you can then at least know how to deal with others.'

Chapter Four – Citizenship | 83

Tan Le

Tan Le's family began planning their escape from Vietnam in 1976, eventually making the break at the end of 1981. They left in a little boat when she was only four years old, and after five days and nights on the open sea were picked up by a British oil tanker off the coast of Malaysia. They stayed in a refugee camp in Malaysia for three months until they were accepted by Australia.

Although no-one in the family knew any English, Tan's mother quickly realised that she didn't want to be stuck working in a factory and she didn't want her children to lack the guidance they would need to help them understand their new society. 'She took up night lessons in English,' says Tan, 'and she would study, pasting little quotes on her machine, and people at work would say, why are you learning like that? You're going to be here for the rest of your life; why are you bothering to learn English?'

Tan grew up in Footscray in Victoria, where she became involved with the Vietnamese Community of Footscray Association, which helps provide training and employment for young Vietnamese Australians. She became President within three years and developed the Australian Vietnamese Services Resource Centre, now recognised as one of the most effective Vietnamese community organisations in Australia.

Tan has organised major cultural events to promote multiculturalism in Melbourne's West and has worked as an effective fundraiser for a number of charities. Her appointments include Member of the Australian Citizenship Council; Member of A Fair Go For All, the National Committee for Human Rights Education; National Ambassador for Aboriginal Reconciliation; and a Member of the Centre for the Mind, Australian National University. In 1998/9 she was Goodwill Ambassador for Australia to Malaysia, Taiwan, China, Thailand and Vietnam. In 1998 she was named Young Australian of the Year.

In 1998 she graduated with Honours in Commerce/Law from Monash University and is now working for the law firm Freehill Hollingdale and Page and is also a regular contributor to the *Vietnamese Weekly*. Awarded a KPMG scholarship in 1997, she is currently developing opportunities for Victorian businesses wanting to trade in Asia.

Mark Leibler AO

On any criteria, Mark Leibler has made an extraordinary contribution to Australia. Following in the footsteps of his father, he has become a leader in the Jewish community and, separately, he is a leader in the legal community in Melbourne and a widely contributing member of the business community. He graduated from Melbourne University Law School in 1966 with an Honours Degree, and in 1968 from Yale University Law School with a Master of Laws with Honours. He is widely published on taxation-related subjects and continues to be invited to lecture and speak in these areas.

Since 1995 he has been President of the United Israel Appeal and, since 1996, National Chairman of the Australia Israel and Jewish Affairs Council. His leadership role extends internationally. He was a member of the executive of the world Zionist organisation from 1988 to 1997 and, since 1992, he has been a governor of the Jewish Agency for Israel.

Mark Leibler's contribution to the community was recognised in his own country when he was awarded the honour of Officer in the General Division of the Order of Australia back in 1987. Internationally he was recognised with the Theodore Herzl Award in recognition of devoted and outstanding service to the Zionist movement.

As the first generation of children whose parents came from Poland and Belgium before the war, he was always conscious of the family history and the need to carry on the family tradition in contributing to the community and respecting education. Almost no sacrifice was too great.

'It wasn't until many years after the war that I really began to understand the significance of what had happened in Europe,' he says. 'There were a million children who were executed in the Nazi death camps, and I think this led to a huge emphasis, on the part of the immigrants, on the importance of children, of nurturing children, almost like making up for this huge loss. 'There was an overwhelming desire on the part of our parents to see that we had what we needed to be happy and to be satisfied and, I think, above all, an emphasis on education and the view that if you're going to make your way in life, this is the key,' he says.

> 'There was an overwhelming desire on the part of our parents to see that we had what we needed to be happy and to be satisfied and, I think, above all, an emphasis on education and the view that if you're going to make your way in life, this is the key.'

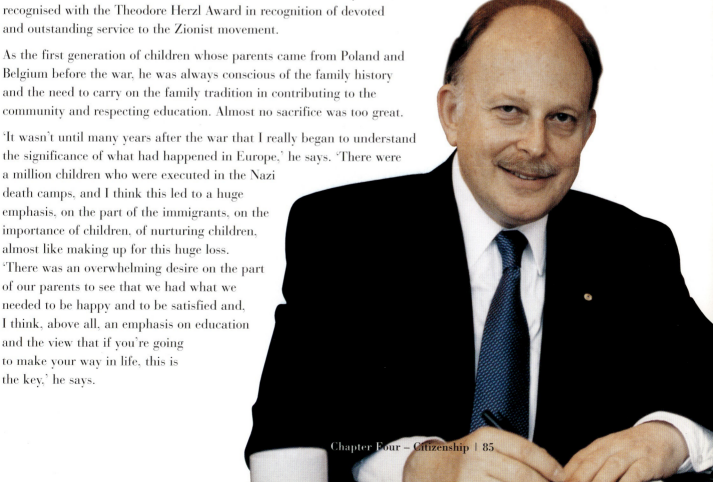

Nelson Leong

Nelson Leong came to Australia in late 1975 because of the war in East Timor. He was carrying a Portuguese passport and considered himself a Portuguese citizen, despite being half Chinese and half Timorese. The Leong family were concerned and frightened of the persecution of the population in east Timor and it was determined that Nelson and his two youngest sisters would leave the country for safety.

The journey was long and terrifying, initially because of the violence in East Timor and then the terror of the responsibility of his two younger sisters, Sally and Jill, and having to remember his mother's instructions, even though he was only 14, about looking after the two little girls. The boat trip was also terrifying, and Nelson was sick with a high fever but still determined to flee to safety. In rough and heavy seas, the Portuguese army carried the women and children on board the ship, their destination Australia.

Nelson Leong didn't choose Australia; he chose safety. Being with his sisters and out of Timor was what mattered. Once on the ship, some thought they were going to Macau, others to Singapore. After two nights and two days they heard they were in Darwin. As they disembarked, a cousin living in Darwin emerged at the wharf, having heard on the grapevine that there were Timorese people arriving. Unfortunately the little Leong clan arrived in Darwin shortly after Cyclone Tracy had flattened the city, and their move into a caravan park shocked them after the life they had left behind.

Darwin was home for four years and the Leong children went to school. Life was tough at school. With little English, and unable to communicate, Nelson was generally considered hopeless academically. But he was good at art and converted his interest in looking at magazines into fashion. After leaving school in Year 11 and taking a year off, Nelson enrolled in a fashion technology course in the Darwin Technology College. He was the first man but was welcomed, and even considered a role model for the males in Darwin. Language and communication were still difficult, but after completing the course, he headed to East Sydney Tech.

In 1984 he graduated from East Sydney Tech and said 'I am really, really, proud that they accepted me because my dream came true.' Nelson's parents came to Australia in 1980 and the family is now in Sydney.

Nelson Leong has been a successful and longstanding independent Sydney designer since opening his first store in 1986. He has an independent Nelson Leong label, sold exclusively through his Sydney stores, and his contribution and commitment to the Australian fashion industry is widely recognised. His clients now come from all over the world.

Chapter Five
What do immigrants value about Australia?

Immigrants from around the world still look to Australia as the land of freedom and opportunity. Those interviewed are clear in expressing their views about Australian values, values they cherish and which they see as definitively Australian.

Freedom of expression comes first. The freedom to say what you think without recrimination is never taken for granted by the newcomer, and the rise of One Nation and its anti-Asian immigrant views was usually seen in this light. The initial fear of racism was steadied by the belief that this was a country that could tolerate such a political party, and that the common denominator in the Australian community would defeat such a party platform.

People spoke about space, and there is a sense that Australia offers space that is both physical and intellectual. Because this is a young European settlement, there is a belief that there is space for new ideas and new ways of doing things and that Australians seem genuinely interested in different solutions. Space to think away from oppressive regimes, space to be creative, for there is a life above survival. These were strong forces even when the newcomers prospered and could have returned to their native lands.

The physical space is also treasured – space to live and space for the children to play. People speak of a landscape so different from the one left behind; different trees and different light, backyards and wide footpaths in the suburbs. While this could be alienating initially, it assumes an importance as an identifier of being Australian. Returning to their first home, immigrants are often shocked at the lack of physical space, the crowded streets and housing and the intense competition for agricultural land. They soon realise how important that sense of space is. Immigrants believe that this is a country where you get a fair go, a place where tolerance and social justice are an integral part of daily life.

Elsa Atkin

Being as far away from Bagdad as I could be, that was a wonderful thing. I guess not feeling that you have to hide things. You try all the time in Bagdad to appeal to their sense of decency, or something like that, by saying, 'Come on, I might be of different background, but look, it's all right. I am pretty okay.' I felt freer here. I could be myself without having to worry about 'what do I have to do?', 'how do I have to walk?', 'how do I have to appear in public?', and stuff like that. We would go to American films every Saturday and Sunday. We wanted to wear exactly the same as the actors were wearing. So you wear those clothes in Bagdad and you get a few young men walking behind you and telling you you are a slut, you are a whore, or things like that.

Tim Besley

I would not be as well off if I'd stayed in New Zealand. The opportunities here are much greater. The other fact is that I think Australia is more laid back, in a good sense. I think New Zealand is still a bit uptight. There are far more diverse influences around – I mean the old steak and eggs days are over. Not quite so much in New Zealand. But I think perhaps there is more determination in the business world here to get things done.

Wolf Blass

I personally think it is a great country. I am in a different position now than I was 25, 30 years ago. It's just the space, the openness of the mentality of the people, their tolerance. And the lifestyle, which has changed, of course, so many times. I would think elitism doesn't really exist, or there is not as apparent an elitism in this country as there is anywhere else.

Paul Boyatzis

I would say the freedom and ability to do whatever you wish to do. No-one can say that there are any obstacles, within reason, in the way of being able to achieve whatever you want, be it academic or professional work. We live in a fortunate world, a free world, a land of opportunity with no restrictions. Again, I am saying, within reason.

Caroline Baum

The ability to dispense most of the time with class as a part of social interaction. I have become much more informal. I have become much more casual. I like that very relaxed way of dealing with people. Then, all sorts of sensual experiences: light, heat, water, intensity of colours, flora, fauna, weird animals, extraordinary food. Everything. I can't think of anything about Australia that I don't enjoy.

Judy Cassab

On my first trip to Alice Springs, when I saw the landscape I knew with absolute certainty why we emigrated. This is my inspiration and it remained my inspiration all those years. It's a spiritual experience, the landscape.

Arlene Chai

What I value now about life in Australia is the sense of freedom that I have and the belief that I can be what I want. I know this is strange, but the sense of space is so different; I mean in Manila it's so congested, there are so many people that I think that affects the way you think as well. But here it's about space and I think that frees up your mind and so you start thinking of possibilities in your life. If I had stayed on in Manila I would never have left advertising and started writing books. I wouldn't have done it because that would not have been an acceptable career path. But here it is.

Chapter Five – What do immigrants value about Australia?

Josef Chromy

The freedom. The personal freedom. You can say what you want, which is very nice. The opportunities. Fixing your goals, if they are not silly goals, which are possible to reach. If you set your cap at goals which should be reachable, you can go and work for them and get there. You can set financial goals and you can work step by step to get to your goal. If it is a small business which has started, it is achievable. Enjoy the benefits and enjoy the quality of the life and enjoy the time and money too – what you can purchase with it. People here sometimes complain, but when I look back, in my country, how long we had to work for anything, for food or whatever, I am very happy.

Diane Grady

Sometimes I love it and sometimes I don't. I call it the 'she'll be right' mentality. David Malouf says that Australians really like to avoid extremes and they very rarely get cross and they dislike murder. I like that; that resistance to extremism is something that is very valuable, and I think that it has led to a certain openness to new things, like technology. We are the quickest adaptors to technology in the world. I think it has led to massive changes in the last 20 years in terms of eating. The changes are awesome when you think about the food, the cosmopolitanisation of food, so I really like that kind of accepting mentality. On the other hand, maybe the side I don't like is the cynicism about people who have achieved something, the cynicism about people who are passionate for anything.

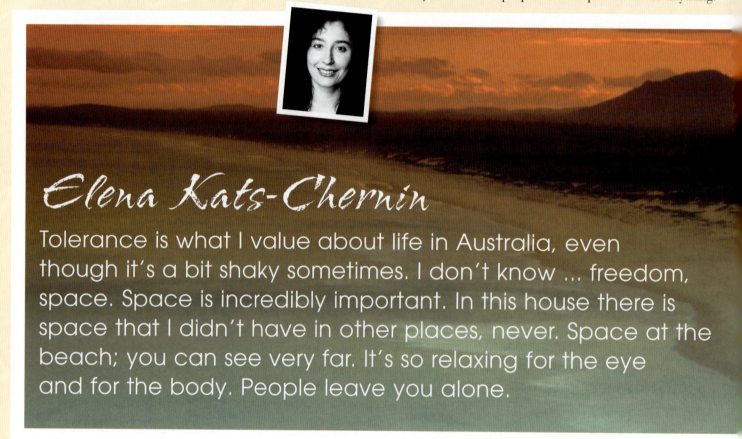

Elena Kats-Chernin

Tolerance is what I value about life in Australia, even though it's a bit shaky sometimes. I don't know ... freedom, space. Space is incredibly important. In this house there is space that I didn't have in other places, never. Space at the beach; you can see very far. It's so relaxing for the eye and for the body. People leave you alone.

Sir James Gobbo

I think my parents valued a sense of opportunity and egalitarianism. We wouldn't, perhaps, call it a 'fair go', but a sense of being able to make one's way in any field. There wasn't any sense that your progress depended on what your family connections were or anything like that. That was, I think, the sense that came through, the sense of satisfaction that they had done it with their own hard work but it was a country that allowed hard work to prosper and to be rewarded. That is something that wasn't always true of the old world.

Akira Isogawa

I love the diversity of the culture. The freedom. The fact that, for instance, if I feel like having a nice meal, if I go out tonight and I feel like having some Indian or maybe the next night I will feel like having something else, like Italian, it is possible. It is very rare. It doesn't happen so much in many countries.

Dai Le

I suppose the freedom to really speak your mind, but sometimes you can't, really. The freedom to have, I think, choice. I can choose not to be a doctor, I can choose not to be a lawyer, which still disappoints my mother. I have got the choice to do what I want, keeping in mind that I have to respect my mother's wishes to a certain point. I have got a job, and I am glad I have a job. What I like is that I am able to go to work every day, have a good quality of life; maybe some Vietnamese people in the community haven't got that.

Judit Korner

What I value about life in Australia is freedom compared to the rest of the world. That vastness, it's really nice. That spaciousness. If you're locked into Paris or New York – we had a choice. There was an opportunity to continue our business and be the Estee Lauders of the world or the Korners of the Australian beauty industry. By then I had children and my husband said 'would you like your children to grow up in New York?' and I thought 'no, not really'. I wouldn't like to live anywhere else. It's nice to be able to travel, and I'm in a fortunate position to be able to do that, but I don't want to live anywhere else.

George Lapaine

Don't forget in 1951 the aftermath of the war was still pretty strong in Europe, and people were desperate. There was no infrastructure; trains weren't running, half the bridges hadn't been re-built. I think coming here to Australia, where really, apart from a little fright in Sydney Harbour with a Japanese sub, they didn't really know what war was all about. I think the availability of food, the open spaces, were things that were very attractive. The fact that there was a chance of doing well for the future, starting from a very hard beginning. The possibility of saving a bit of money and buying a house eventually. That was the big ambition that all our friends had.

Tan Le

That sense of freedom and space are still real for me: the space is not just physical space. When we first came it was purely physical space that made a first impression on me, but there's so much room for opportunity, room to be different and yet you can still belong. I have just come back from a trip to Asia and I think the space has made a tremendous difference to our family. And the freedom to have your own beliefs, to have your own voice and to be heard if you want to be heard. It's something that we could not possibly have anywhere else.

Lou Klepac

I like the space. Australia, for a long time, was the Switzerland in a time of war. Nice, peaceful and quiet, and it wasn't dangerous. When the war finished you went back to Paris and you went back to London because you jumped into life. In a way you think 'wouldn't it be rather nice to live half your life in Paris and Venice and so on?' But, of course, my children are here.

Magda Wollner

I value the Australian way of freedom and the sense of humour which is mixed up with it. I went to London with a wonderful friend who had an Australian passport. I had a British one. She was absolutely disgusted with me that I, as a B.F. – a bloody foreigner – went straight through immigration and she had to queue up for an hour with her Australian passport.

Nelson Leong

Freedom. I think the freedom that Australians have is unlike any other country in the world. Not even America can come close. I think Australians care for freedom, Australians care for the environment, Australians care about poverty, Australians have got good hearts. If you look generally at Australia, we contribute a lot to other countries. We donate a lot to other countries. We always want to be part of some other people's business, like war and poverty, not because we want to be involved but because we care. We can't stay back and watch people die or people starve. Australian people have actually got hearts. That is what I think.

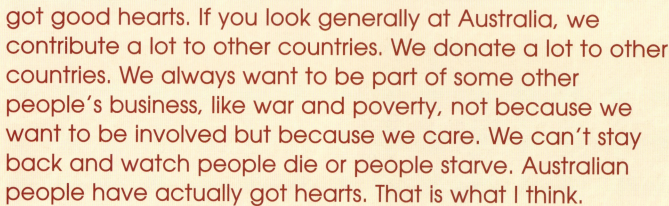

Mark Leibler

What my father prized about Australia, bearing in mind where we came from, was that it was a land of freedom, a land of opportunity, a land where one could express oneself without fear of retribution, a land which had the potential for a wonderful education system which was open to all. It was a very relaxed form of living, free of violence and violent pressures, and free of the shrill sort of denunciations and discriminations and actions that were taking place in Europe. It was like a haven. And that explains why, if you look at areas of charitable giving, whether it's the arts, hospitals, whatever it is, you'll find members of the Jewish community figuring disproportionately amongst the donors. It's because many of those Jews are immigrants, or the children of immigrants.

Juliana Nkrumah

What do I value most about Australia? Maybe what is not there. We are a country and we have no national identity per se. I am looking for a nationalism. So I am looking to value, probably, a dream. A nationalism, a sense of the nation that I can hold on to. There are so many of us from various nations and I suppose it is a dream, because we can't have a nationalism when we have all come from various nations. But if we could forge one, we could be a force to contend with. I want to be proud of being Australian, but unfortunately my colour and my looks do not allow me to be absorbed into that identity easily. I have known for a long time I will be on the fringes and so will my children, and that is very unfortunate for my children.

George Mure

The opportunities have been absolutely brilliant here. Wonderful lifestyle. I mean the competition for anything you do in Europe is fiendish, and you need a lot more money to kick it off. You come up with an idea here and there are still opportunities. We have got everything here. There are great opportunities. You've just got to think laterally a bit sometimes. There is nowhere to compare with it.

Sir Arvi Parbo

I think the freedom, really, as compared to the countries I went to before I came here; particularly during the war, there were all sorts of restrains and checks. Under the Soviet system you couldn't change the place where you lived without going and registering. You had a pass, and every time you changed your job it had to be registered and approved. When you changed wherever you lived, a room, flat, house or whatever it was, that had to be all changed and you had to be re-registered. All this sort of thing. You were very tightly controlled. Of course in Germany after the war, in the refugee camps, you were really constrained in what you could do.

Rolando Ramos

I value the freedom. I value the option of meeting so many different people. I still find it quite rich in that sense. I still value, and I still get excited, going out into the street and seeing so many different faces. In the last few years there have been lots of forces that go against that and that is a bit of a sad moment for me to see how some people cannot really see how this is so enriching for everyone.

Chapter Five – What do immigrants value about Australia? | 95

Dagmar Schmidmaier

I think the opportunity to start afresh. I think my mother really valued that equality, that you could come here and do anything you wanted to do if you put your mind to it. So although she chose, through a range of circumstances, to do home duties and cleaning, she always instilled in me that education was going to provide the opportunities. There was a really strong assumption that I would go to university and that I would have a professional life of some sort. She had this vision that I should be a doctor.

Jim Trambas

I guess the openness and the help I got as a newcomer here from people I didn't know. My neighbours, my friends, went out of their way to help me. Not by feeling sorry for me, but because they wanted to learn about my culture. The way we eat, the way we work, the way we behave, the way we get crabby, the way we boss our women around, the way they boss us around. It was an interesting environment at the time and it was amazing. I guess if I had met them in Greece I would have done the same, but everything fell into place as far as fitting in with other people.

Ngoc Trang Thomas

We valued the lifestyle. It is peaceful and the people more open; it's just a relaxed Australian way of life. If we had stayed in France or England we would not have the lifestyle, and if we had stayed in, say, the United States – Canada would have been our second choice, but we didn't like the weather. My sister was in Toronto then, and I didn't like the weather, so Australia had everything. People don't appreciate and realise how lucky we are. Even now I think Australia is still one of the best places we have at the moment; high unemployment and all the problems, but compared to the rest of world I think it is still the best place.

'In terms of cultural identity, the fact that I am Chinese is very high up, and being born and raised in Hong Kong is also an important part of my identity.'

Dr Anita Mak

Dr Anita Mak graduated as a Bachelor of Social Science from Hong Kong University in 1975. Two years later she got her Masters in Social Science. She arrived in Canberra as the spouse of a PhD student at the Australian National University and worked there for a year as a research assistant until she started doing her own PhD. Because of her husband's sponsorship agreement they returned to Hong Kong, but both decided to emigrate. At the end of 1984, they arrived back in Canberra, where she resumed her studies. In 1988 she was awarded a Doctor of Philosophy from the Australian National University. Her discipline is applied psychology and she currently holds the position of senior lecturer in Applied Psychology at the University of Canberra.

Being part of a close-knit graduate student community and getting support from people from all parts of the world, Anita had little trouble settling in to life in Canberra which, she says, they fell in love with straight away.

She became an Australian citizen in 1987 in a ceremony held on Australia Day in the National Library.

'I think it is an important passage,' she says. 'It shows an identity. I have a number of identities, and being an Australian is an important one, but it's not my sole identity. It's my priority identity. In terms of cultural identity, the fact that I am Chinese is very high up, and being born and raised in Hong Kong is also an important part of my identity. Being a psychologist, being a researcher, being a woman, being a mother and so on, a whole range of identities.'

Anita's current research interests are cross-cultural adaptation, stress and coping and adolescent deviance and health. She is committed to building bridges for people across cultures so that they can achieve their career and study goals and become socially effective citizens.

She has received a teaching award for innovative teaching and the University of Canberra's award for service to the University in the area of women's career development. She is also the associate editor of the *Australian Journal of Psychology* and sub-editor of *International Education Electronic Journal*.

'They were dead against me being a fisherman but the call of the sea won out.'

George Mure

No visit to Tasmania is complete without a meal at Mures. When the Tall Ships gathered at Constitution Dock in 1988, Mures was the point of convergence. 'See you at Mures' was expressed in many languages, and the line was learned quickly.

George Mure was a child of the war years in England. He lived a comfortable life with his family in Norfolk until his mother remarried and went to live in Kenya. In Norfolk and Kenya, George had access to boats and fishing. In East Africa he spent hours swimming and fishing at a fishery owned by family friends.

'It was in Kenya that I really got interested in fish,' he says. 'I used to go down to the East Africa Fisheries and go out on the boats. I have never lost that interest in fish. In fact, as a schoolboy, I won a natural history prize in Kenya for painting fish.'

When the family returned to the United Kingdom, George's stepfather, a doctor, twisted his arm and made him study medicine. 'It was the most ridiculous thing because I faint at the sight of blood anyway, so it was never going to work. They were dead against me being a fisherman but the call of the sea won out.' He signed on as a deckie learner with a North Sea trawler.

Meeting his future wife, Jill, changed his life. Jill came from a family whose father managed Scotts, a well-known top quality seafood restaurant. She worked there through her long student holidays and developed her passion for seafood and restaurants.

In 1962 they married and sailed for Australia a week later. Within a month of arriving in Sydney, George was sent to Hobart to buy and sell fish for a fish marketing company. The Mures lived in Melbourne and Perth, working in the fishing industry until they saved enough money to buy their first boat, a 42ft crayboat with a six ton freezer. Life and work fishing in Geraldton, Darwin, Cairns and New Guinea, and producing two children, did not make them rich but gave them wonderful insights to Australia and Australians. They lived an adventurous life and when George damaged his knee and was told to give up life on boats they followed their next dream of opening a fish restaurant. This they did in Tasmania and Mures Fish House opened in 1973. Mures at Constitution Dock came in the 1980s.

Prof Satendra Nandan

Satendra Nandan is the elected international chair of the Association of the Commonwealth Literature and Language Studies and the Director of the Canberra Centre for Writing and Cultural Studies at the University of Canberra. He lectures in Commonwealth Literature and Creative Communication at the university.

Born in Fiji on the banks of the Nandi River, he grew up in the village of Votualevu by Nadi airport. His grandparents had migrated under the indenture system from the United Provinces in India to the Fijian archipelago in the 1890s to work on the sugarcane plantations owned by the CSR company of Australia.

Satendra completed his primary and secondary education in Fiji and was subsequently educated, under various awards, at the universities of Delhi, Leeds, London and the Australian National University in Canberra, where he completed his doctorate on the fiction of Patrick White. He says he 'discovered' Australia through White's novels, first read in a hotel in London in the early seventies. He's currently co-translating the Nobel Laureate's *The Tree Of Man* into Hindi.

At the inception of the University of the South Pacific in Fiji, he was appointed a lecturer in English, and taught there until April 1987 when he became a minister in the Bavadra Cabinet. He left Fiji in December 1987 after the two Fijian coups to take up a fellowship at the Humanities Research Centre, ANU. Satendra was Fiji's first Labour Member of Parliament and was deeply involved in the academic, cultural and political issues of Fiji's multiethnic, plural society. He was elected to Parliament in 1982 and again in 1987.

Satendra's work reflects his deep commitment to multiculturalism, human rights, creative writing, ethics and deomocratic politics. Besides half a dozen books, he has contributed over 100 articles and papers on linguistic, literary, cultural, political and human rights issues central to the multiple concerns of post-colonial polity. His creative and critical work is internationally recognised and he has been a recipient of grants, fellowships and awards that have enabled him to write about India, Australia and Fiji, including his autobiography, *Requiem for a Rainbow: An Indian-Fijian Journey*. He is also writing a novel set in Fiji, Canberra and New Delhi and a volume entitled *Indian Fragments*.

Satendra is a member of the ACT Cultural Council and chairs its Literature Committee; he is an elected executive member of the Word Festival, Canberra and has been a judge for the Commonwealth Prize for Fiction.

He lives in Canberra with his wife Jyoti and three children.

Juliana Nkrumah

Juliana Nkrumah was born and raised in Ghana and lived in Zimbabwe for six years. She, her husband and their first daughter arrived in Australia on a Ghanaian passport in 1988. The journey was prompted by her husband's opportunity to study at the University of New South Wales. Both highly educated, Juliana completed her Master's Degree in Social Sciences in 1987 from the University of Zimbabwe.

Despite her education and good English, the people in her community said she should work in a factory to help support her husband and daughter. Her first job, as a finishing hand in a dry cleaning factory, gave her eczema and she cried every day for the five months she was there. It didn't stop her from applying for more than a hundred jobs, from which she received only two serious responses.

The breakthrough came when she was hired as a welfare worker by the Anglican Home Mission Society and was assigned to case work in the Kings Cross, Darlinghurst and Surry Hills areas. As one of the welfare workers doing intake at the Surry Hills drop-in centre in Albion Street, she tried to set up a support activity for women who were on drugs and those who were on the streets.

'It was a very interesting place to work because most of our clients were people who were alcohol and drug dependent,' she says. 'Some of them were

100 | A Fair Go – Portraits of the Australian Dream

discriminatory, but some of them were amazingly – I was the only black worker there – respectful.' Because she was theoretically trained in Social Sciences, she had no practical experience and was constantly shocked by what she saw. After a year she moved to Marrickville Care Force Centre. It was there that she began to work with refugees and asylum seekers and joined ANCCORW (Australian National Consultative Committee on Refugee Women) as Committee Member and later as the Convenor. Juliana's work with female circumcision began with her position as publicist and fundraiser for IWDA (International Women's Development Agency) in Sydney from 1992 through 1993, and her community activism with ACC (African Communities Council) in Sydney. She was asked by IWDA to bring together a group of Africans to meet with the President of the Inter Africa Committee Against Harmful Traditional Practices (IAC), who was in Australia from Geneva for a conference. Subsequently she applied for the position of Community Education Coordinator on Female Genital Mutilation with the Ethnic Affairs Commission in New South Wales.

Sir Arvi Parbo AC

Sir Arvi Parbo was born in Tallinn, Estonia, and received his early education there. When the Soviet Union annexed the Baltic States in 1940 there followed deportations, arrests and executions of community leaders. In 1941, when Hitler attacked the Soviet Union, Estonia fell under German occupation, which lasted for three years. When the fortunes of war reversed and the Germans retreated, Estonia once more fell to the victorious Soviets.

'Many people, including myself, preferred not to live under the Soviet system,' says Sir Arvi. 'Some of them who had access to boats fled to Sweden; those who didn't took the land route and finished up in Germany. I was one of those who finished up in Germany, so when the war ended I was a refugee.' Sir Arvi's family also tried to leave, but they left their run too late and were overtaken by the Red Army and turned back.

Sir Arvi attended the Clausthal Mining Academy in Germany from 1946 to 1948. 'During the vacations I worked in mines, partly to get experience, partly to earn money,' he says. 'I became aware, during my underground experience, that there really wasn't much future for young mining engineers in Germany because the industry was not expanding.'

The options open to him at the time included migration to England, which wanted mainly farm workers, Canada, the United States and Australia. Canada and the United States had fairly lengthy immigration procedures, but Australia was actively canvassing in Europe's refugee camps for young, healthy people. And there was little bureaucratic fuss. Knowing that if he applied and passed the health requirements he would be in Australia in a matter of months, and attracted by Australia's mining industry, Sir Arvi applied.

Life in Australia began in a migrant camp in Adelaide, where he was sent to work in a quarry, using a jackhammer to drill holes in rocks which were then filled with explosives. Anxious to return to university and finish his course, he was admitted to the University of Adelaide in early 1951. In his third year he was given a Mature Age Scholarship, which allowed him to study full-time. He graduated with a Bachelor of Engineering Degree with First Class Honours in 1955, and looks back on those years as the time he began to think of himself as an Australian.

Communication with his family in Estonia had been difficult throughout that time, and it was not until 1969 that he returned to visit his parents, his brothers and 'three thousand other relations of all kinds'.

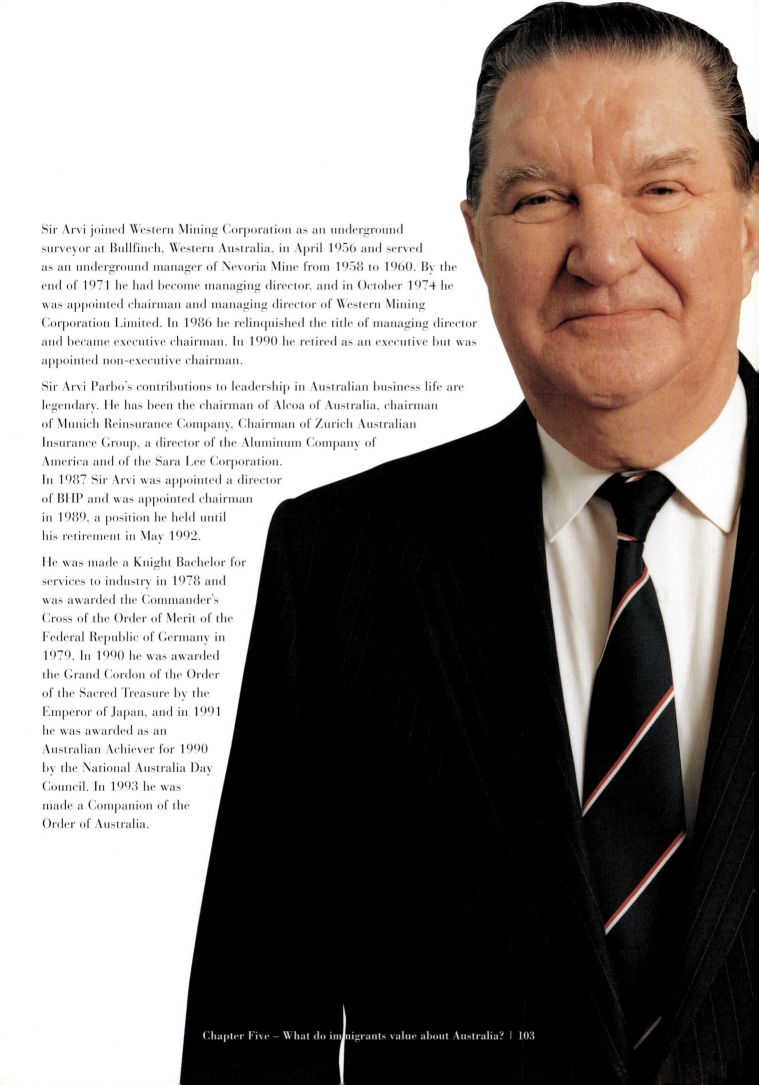

Sir Arvi joined Western Mining Corporation as an underground surveyor at Bullfinch, Western Australia, in April 1956 and served as an underground manager of Nevoria Mine from 1958 to 1960. By the end of 1971 he had become managing director, and in October 1974 he was appointed chairman and managing director of Western Mining Corporation Limited. In 1986 he relinquished the title of managing director and became executive chairman. In 1990 he retired as an executive but was appointed non-executive chairman.

Sir Arvi Parbo's contributions to leadership in Australian business life are legendary. He has been the chairman of Alcoa of Australia, chairman of Munich Reinsurance Company, Chairman of Zurich Australian Insurance Group, a director of the Aluminum Company of America and of the Sara Lee Corporation. In 1987 Sir Arvi was appointed a director of BHP and was appointed chairman in 1989, a position he held until his retirement in May 1992.

He was made a Knight Bachelor for services to industry in 1978 and was awarded the Commander's Cross of the Order of Merit of the Federal Republic of Germany in 1979. In 1990 he was awarded the Grand Cordon of the Order of the Sacred Treasure by the Emperor of Japan, and in 1991 he was awarded as an Australian Achiever for 1990 by the National Australia Day Council. In 1993 he was made a Companion of the Order of Australia.

Chapter Six
Multi-
culturalism

'I cannot think of a better place in the entire world, a more shining example of how people come together as one nation and one community than Sydney, Australia,' said United States President, Bill Clinton, when he visited Australia in 1997.

Chairman of the Ethnic Affairs Commission of New South Wales, Stepan Kerkyasharian's address to the Sydney Institute in 1994, *The Paradox of Australian Multiculturalism*, reminds us that multiculturalism is a word which is asked to do a number of different jobs, and that fact is often advanced as a reason for getting rid of it. In reality, multiculturalism is both a public policy and a demographic fact. According to Kerkyasharian: 'Assimilation was presented as a failure when migrant alienation started showing up, and it led to three important understandings which shaped multiculturalism as we know it today. These were:

We cannot ask people to surrender their identity. Language, culture and identity are indivisible. Change should be allowed to happen naturally, rather than be forced upon an unwilling migrant population.

We have a public duty to ensure that people get equality of treatment.

Cultural diversity is an asset to be fostered in the national interest, rather than a problem we have to overcome.

We have here the three underlying tenets that shape the policy of multiculturalism: cultural identity, which is simply the right to be yourself; social justice, which is simply a fair go; and economic benefit, which means simply that new people can offer new ways of dealing with old problems.'

The question about multiculturalism is whether it is an expression or an agent of social change. Kerkyasharian maintains that 'the largest share of the credit for the success of multiculturalism lies not with Australian institutions, government, or the public service, but with the people of Australia.

'I think there is something in our national character and social traditions which helps to explain our paradox and makes me optimistic about the future,' he said.

The people profiled here support this view of multiculturalism. The right to acknowledge your cultural heritage, while identifying yourself as an Australian, is cherished. Inclusiveness is the future.

Elsa Atkin

Multiculturalism means different cultures living harmoniously. Identifying with the major culture, with the core culture of a country, but holding on to some elements of their own culture to give them that continuity. It is important that you hold on to some of your heritage for psychological reasons. Multiculturalism for me is that you hold on to some elements of your culture, but the major thing that you identify with, that ties you together, that ties you to the country, is that core culture that you hold yourself.

Tim Besley

I don't like the word multicultural. I've never liked it because I think we're all Australians. Multiculturalism, to me, indicates a chopping up into pieces of the Australian nation into different cultural groups. Now I don't say that they shouldn't keep their cultural heritage and their cultural skills, but I think we can all learn from each other. Multiculturalism to me says there are Greeks and there are Italians and Germans, whereas my view is that we are all Australians from different cultural backgrounds. Multiculturalism has passed its use-by date.

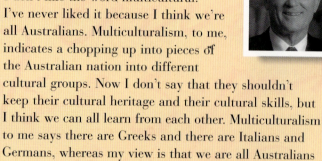

Petro Georgiou

Multiculturalism essentially means that we have done two things. One, we have recognised as a nation that to be an Australian you don't have to reject everything else – your heritage, your language. It also means that we are a society that not only tolerates, but also respects diversity, both on an individual level and in terms of its contribution to the nation as a whole. That's what multiculturalism means to me. It does symbolise a commitment. I always get fixated whenever people start speaking about 'cosmopolitanism' as an alternative. I keep thinking about Stalin and the attack on cosmopolitanism. Cosmopolitanism actually means ruthlessness and a lack of commitment. That is not what multiculturalism means. Multiculturalism is a commitment to Australia with a recognition that we are a diverse society. Once again, it does have its roots in a rejection of assimilation.

Mala Dharmananda

At a personal level, for me multiculturalism is annoying, because it brings out the worst of people wearing national costume on independence day, eating traditional food, a static culture. Multiculturalism emphasises a particular notion of culture over other issues to do with ethnicity and to do with religion, for which there is little space in Australian public discourse. Having said that, I do appreciate that multiculturalism has been an attempt on the part of government public policy to give everyone an opportunity to express who they are. I just don't like the concept.

Vivi Germanos-Koutsounadis

I see the fact that people from so many different countries of the world are working together, living together, participating together to make this country what it is. The blend. I think we are fortunate to have so many people from so many different parts of the world coming here voluntarily. Others not, you know, like the refugees who have no choice. Coming here voluntarily, contributing all these cultural, religious, arts, thoughts, ideologies, politics and blending and making it the unique aspect that is Australia.

Sir James Gobbo

I made a speech in which I said that by the end of the 1990s I hoped that we would have stopped using the word 'multiculturalism'. I thought the word, in a truly multicultural society, was unnecessary. If, in fact, those principles applied, it should be so much part of the tapestry of society that you wouldn't need to have an 'ism' that described it. You would simply know that this is what being an Australian is all about.

Diane Grady

If you think that it is okay to kill somebody just because they don't agree with you and that's part of your religion or your basic philosophy, then I don't value multiculturalism. So I think that we should be a lot clearer with basic values that people should be asked to sign up for before migrating here. I don't think that we should have people who believe that, by virtue of your sex, you are unequal. That is a pretty strong statement, and that would leave out a few cultures. I just feel that we should welcome people of any colour, any race, religion, whatever, as long as they support some basic values.

Akira Isogawa

I think I like that word very much. I think it presents Australia really well, that word itself. I am glad to be part of it. It is a really exciting word.

Bill Jegorow

Australia has always been multicultural, even before European settlement. Multiculturalism is also a policy, to my way of thinking, which should provide equality of opportunity and, hopefully, some equity in outcome. That is something that is reasonably recent, because multiculturalism was not acknowledged before the 1970s. In fact it was Al Grassby who imported the word from Canada.

Ted Johnson

Multiculturalism means you can have ethnic origins and you don't have to give them up when you come to Australia. You might, you should become an Australian citizen, you should vote in Australia, you should contribute to Australian life, not just economically, but you should also have, and should be encouraged to have, a sense of pride about where you come from as well as where you're going. So I think multiculturalism is all about the feeling of identity in the wider sense but a feeling of pride about how you came to be here.

Chapter Six – Multiculturalism | 107

Lou Klepac

Everyone must assimilate. You want an Australia made up of Australians. I think it is a big mistake to allow Croatians or Turks to live here but to think of Croatia as their home. I may be Croatian, I may be Triesteen or Venetian, but my allegiance is to my house. I don't want to arrange a marriage for my daughter, or keep the traditions of a previous country. It is a big mistake. I would allow migrants to come in and, after 10 years, I would give them an English test. If they didn't speak the language I would send them back to where they came from because they are not interested in becoming part of this country.

Ted Kunkel

I just think there is so much strength and depth in sharing cultures and blending cultures that it just gives Australia an opportunity, almost like America had, to really do it and get it right. I think the concept of integration and multiculturalism is just fantastic.

George Lapaine

I think having been through assimilation, where people said, 'Look, if you don't fit in, piss off', multiculturalism was such a revolution. I think it gave pride to a lot of people. I think it was the best thing that ever happened. I know people grow impatient with words and I know there has been a movement to knock multiculturalism in the last year or so, but to me it is the best thing that has ever happened in Australia. I think it has given people a sort of sense of pride and a sense that they could still be 'wogs' and be accepted.

Dai Le

I like the concept of it, but I think it has been misused quite a bit. It is a shame because it does describe Australia. I remember when I first heard it it was quite an innocent word, but I think it is not what it is meant to be now. I don't think we are using it to describe the diversity and the richness of society.

Tan Le

I don't think of the word 'multicultural' as such. I think it denotes a certain reality of Australia. It's the same as other 'isms', you either hate them passionately or you like them passionately. To me multiculturalism is only a word used to describe something. It doesn't conjure up anything for me. It doesn't have a special meaning. That's the nature of Australia; it's a multicultural society. I believe more in the reality of it than in the word.

Judit Korner

The whole world is multicultural. Is there such a thing as a pure anything? There isn't. If you look back where I come from this happens all the time. Look, they're killing each other next door to me. The Hungarian youths are sent to the border, to Yugoslavia. Don't people ever learn? Fortunately it hasn't happened here. So my mother's foresight of being a long way away, so far, has worked. Just because someone has different-coloured skin, a different religion and different beliefs from me, do I have to destroy them? The world is big enough to carry all of us.

Mark Leibler

I think multicultural is a great word. I think there's a real problem about shunning the word, because it sends a message around the place. Multicultural means that we are a land with a multiplicity of cultures, but that doesn't prevent us from working together and being Australians at one and the same time and developing as an overlay to those multicultural traditions an Australian cultural tradition as well. They are not mutually inconsistent.

Anita Mak

I think the potential of the power of diversity is tremendous. I'm really enlightened by how it's been embraced by some political leaders and certainly some business leaders. I am also saddened by the fact that it doesn't mean a lot to ordinary people on the street. I'm not sure how to bridge that gap, but that gap has to be bridged. There has to be a commitment to really helping culturally different Australians to be socially effective. Sometimes people's confidence is being undermined, especially by the physical differences which bring out the cultural differences very prominently, and in my interaction with people that's very often the first thing that comes across. It takes them a little while to realise that okay, I'm beyond my different looks. I'm not just an Asian. And that applies to everybody. We are not just one identity, and that is true of gender, age, dress. It's something that has to be recognised.

George Mure

Australia has done it very, very well, I think. I think it is absolutely vital that people think of themselves, certainly from the second generation onwards, as Australians. I think the problem with multiculturalism is ghettos. If you get ghettos, you get problems. You must have people that assimilate. I am being a terrible optimist when I say that. We have friends with many genetic, I suppose you could say, backgrounds, but one generation down I reckon you are Australian. I consider myself Australian first generation down but a lot of people can't do that, especially non-English speaking people.

Satendra Nandan

The thing that appeals to me most about Australia is its diverse multiculturalism. It has recognised that you are very much a part of a world that is diverse, plural and of infinite variety, and that your life story is as important as my life story or my knowledge of a particular religious ceremony or right is as important as anyone else's. This is a very post-colonial thing. If you go in search of the source of the river, even the Murrumbidgee, you don't find a single source: you find millions of sources. And human beings are like that. If I went back I would find that Hindus, Muslims, Christians, Turks are all part of my inheritance.

Juliana Nkrumah

Multiculturalism as I have seen it to this point has meant bring your food, bring your dance, bring your festivities, bring your colour and let's toss it all together. You know, like a salad that is coloured differently but is beautiful, but in that salad you can identify the capsicum. So long as it's food, it's carnivale, it's all that language that we can use for business and other things, we are okay. Only when it comes to sharing the pie, there are people who can have a big share and there are the rest of us who cannot and will be asked to stay on the fringes.

Gladys Roach

I guess to me it is a word that describes the mix of society that we have and the way of life that we have. When we came to Australia, food was always a piece of meat and three boiled vegetables, and curry was always the leftover Sunday roast with a spoon of curry powder, and whatever was available in the supermarket with fruit and jam, or whatever, was put on it. Now I really believe that Australia has the best food in the whole world.

Neville Roach

I think a question that people often ask, or if they don't ask they must think about, is the whole issue of loyalty. 'Are you an Indian at heart, or are you an Australian at heart?' I think that's an important question. The answer, I think, is that you end up being both. I think that's what's good about multiculturalism – it says you can be both and that's okay.

Sir Arvi Parbo

I don't like the word 'multiculturalism' because I think the word has acquired many different meanings on both sides, by those who use it and those who listen to it. I wish they would think of a different single word, because it has really outlived its usefulness. There is no question about the idea. Just a society, a community, where people have come from hundreds of different countries. It is absolutely free. You can do whatever you like. You can talk your own language. You can listen to your own radio programs.

Rolando Ramos

I think I am pro-multiculturalism. I think multiculturalism as a word has become a bit misused, especially by politicians. Politicians misuse and use multiculturalism as a way of buying votes. I think the concept of multiculturalism, or a multi-racial society, for instance, is a fantastic concept. I feel part of it. In many ways I am quite active in fighting to promote it. But when it comes to something like a political football, then multiculturalism as a word, as a concept, becomes quite different.

Sarina Russo

Multiculturalism means to me that Australians understand that we live in a global village, that everyone today has some special quality and some special culture that we can integrate in our community and enjoy the different cultures. As a child I didn't experience that. I was having dinner with a Greek boy and I was saying that in my early years I had an enormous challenge with the culture, even the food. You know Parmesan cheese was something you just sneered at, and garlic as well. If I ever had any Australian girlfriends, they'd never want to eat at my house. Yet I love Italian food. I can recall, vividly, my sister, who is two and a half years older than me, sharing our sandwiches away from the Australian kids because we had salami. All I dreamed of was Vegemite and peanut paste.

Fred Shahin

We have to respect each other regardless of colour, or race, or whatever. It also means that you should be broadminded to the point that the process of melting together as one nation – we should be more open to one another and take good habits from one another. Not all Australian habits are good, and Australians should not expect immigrants, particularly educated immigrants, to throw away 6000 years of written history and forget all about it just because they arrived here. That's too much to ask. We have something to offer inasmuch as we are open to learn, to accept, or at least try. We have very healthy food; there is the English cuisine, the French cuisine, Italian food, Greek food. Australian food is a combination. Australia is now like a pregnant woman in her seventh or eighth month.

Caroline Baum

Yes, 'multiculturalism' is a good word. It is something that you have to keep testing in yourself. You have to keep asking yourself, 'Do I ever have a prejudicial relationship with anyone? Do I ever get annoyed because a taxi driver doesn't speak enough English to me or can't read an address properly? Am I absolutely impeccable as far as my multiculturalism goes?' I think I have a long way to go and a lot to learn.

Paul Boyatzis

Today I think you can say we are Australians of Anglo-Saxon background, of Aboriginal background, of Greek background and so on.

Judy Cassab

I am not uncomfortable with the word 'multicultural'. I remember how difficult it was. I wanted the children to keep speaking Hungarian to us, or even German. They refused. They were six and four years old and they would not answer us in Hungarian so we had to give it up. So it wasn't enough that we cooked differently and that we had accents; even speaking Hungarian to them was impossible. I don't know whether, later, they wished they had learnt it. It is not an important language to have except they would never know their father is a great wit because you can't make puns in a language you learn.

Wolf Blass

I think we have to be very careful, since this country has never experienced an ageing population. We are reaching for the first time an ageing population, and the government is not prepared. They haven't any foresight about how to handle people when they retire and the question must be asked: 'Where does our social contribution go? To the old people who have been here their whole lives? Or do we support people who have not really contributed to the growth of this country?'

Chapter Six – Multiculturalism | 113

Dagmar Schmidmaier

I believe if you come with an attitude that says, 'I want to contribute to this society', rather than 'What can I get from this society?', that is really important. I sometimes look at what is happening now, the promotion of difference rather than the promotion of how we can meld our cultures together. Simply by coming here you are changing. You are changing the way you look at things. Even the language changes in the way it is modified. I honestly believe there should be a much greater emphasis on pulling together and celebrating those things that we value within the Australian context, rather than such a very strong push to try and change the Australian context to meet very parochial interest groups who are pushing very strongly.

Con Sciacca

Australia is a place where we practise cultural diversity. We have over 200 cultures making up Australian culture and helping us move towards an identity of what that is. I am not sure that we really know who we are at the moment, but that does not matter too much. We are moving towards knowing it. But we are practising a cultural diversity. We can value the culture we left behind while embracing the new, and that is a wonderful opportunity.

Paul Simons

I don't use the word 'multicultural'. I don't know what my attitude to that is. I think everyone that I run into, whether it's a Greek or Italian businessman or Chinese traders or Indian people who have settled here in Australia, I just regard them as Australian. I know that they have their own cultures in their groups, but I don't see that as being obtrusive in any way. I think it's very nice. They go to their Greek churches or Indian temples or mosques, so what?

Jim Spigelman

It means a recognition of an integrated community where persons do not need to deny their origins in order to fully participate. They have the option of continuing to identify with the community in all or some respects but they are not obliged to assimilate in that way, denying their origins, in order to not only operate effectively in the community but also to succeed in the community.

Ngoc Trang Thomas

I think multiculturalism is a policy of acknowledgment that people who come to Australia can keep their heritage, can be assisted in maintaining their traditions and anything that is important to them. However, I also believe that multiculturalism also emphasises the fact that we are here as Australians. We should pledge loyalty to Australia first and we should be Australians first.

Jim Trambas

I think multiculturalism is exciting. The introduction of some new races into society creates a few initial problems. We have brought, say, a lot of Vietnamese people here, and instead of putting them in the right place and giving them a job of work we have built 12-storey flats in Melbourne to put them in. I think that bit is difficult. When we came there were opportunities, the government gave us opportunities. I don't believe we should bring people here and put them in 12-storey buildings and lock them in there.

Agnes Whiten

Multiculturalism is a great concept, but I must qualify that. I am a member of the National Multicultural Advisory Council. The problem with the word is in communicating it to the wider community. Multiculturalism is a beautiful concept; we all have to embrace it. But before I embrace anything, just like the way I was before I became an Australian, I had to be committed. That's my view of Australia.

Wilson Wu

As far as multiculturalism is concerned, it is a wonderful concept. We are Australians and we value our heritage. We can coexist without feeling bad about the past we have left behind, yet we are integrated and in the Australian mainstream. When I first heard Hanson's words I thought 'Oh no, not again. Please don't let me live in a country where I'm going to feel alienated.' It was an ugly moment, but then there was the affirmation that Australia is a very stable democracy, where different views and dissenting views can be expressed. And indeed I would say that Australia has taught me to be more tolerant and accepting.

Rolando Ramos

Rolando Ramos was born in Chile and arrived in Australia in 1987. He had graduated from the University of Chile Drama Department, completing a Bachelor of Arts/Drama degree. In 1986 he founded a professional theatre group, Triquinuela-La, which explored new forms of theatrical experience in relation to space, the audience and subject matters.

His journey to Australia was basically for political reasons, and he arrived here under a program called 'The Humanitarian Program', which allowed people with political problems in Chile to immigrate to Australia. The first stop for this young political refugee was the Villawood Migrant Hostel. It was to be the transition point between the past and the new life, and he and his wife were there for over three months. For Rolando, the sense of space after the confines of Chile was wonderfully liberating. The couple has a son who was born in Australia a year after they arrived here.

He spoke no English when he arrived and was anxious that he would not be able to work as an actor or theatre facilitator, but he made rapid progress in the hostel-run English language classes. A Chilean actor who had lived here for some years helped him find his way into the industry, first with Spanish companies and directors working in Sydney, moving gradually into English-language productions. While working as a factory hand and teaching drama to the Spanish community Rolando auditioned for a part in one episode of the television series, *A Country Practice*. From that he did an episode of *Rafferty's Rules*.

'After I finished with those episodes on television I had to find a job,' he says. 'It just happened that Sidetrack Performers Group was doing auditions and I got into that with my very broken English. I worked with Sidetrack for about eight years, and that gave me a lot of exposure in the industry and it gave me a big chance to be able to break that fear of speaking English, of not being able to perform.'

Since 1991, he has been active in the Multicultural Theatre Alliance, assisting in the MTA Festivals. His work now encompasses film, computer animation, music and sound composition, production skills and directing programs for ABC and SBS radio.

Gladys Roach

Gladys Roach was born in Mangalore, India, and arrived as a new bride in Adelaide in 1965. She was, in her own words, 'a rich spoilt daughter with an indulgent father' and, prior to marriage, had graduated with an Honours degree in Arts from the University of Bombay. Growing up in a household of servants, she had no domestic skills and was completely unprepared for life as a wife on a restricted budget. Her neighbours showed her how to wash clothes and shop in supermarkets. If she wanted to eat Indian food she had to cook it, and even finding ingredients was difficult, especially in Adelaide.

Pregnancy almost immediately restricted her ability to do casual teaching, but pride would not permit asking for financial help from India, and she would pose in front of other people's cars and houses to be photographed to send images home that indicated she and her husband Neville (opposite) were doing well. There was an expectation that all people who lived overseas were successful, and she didn't want to disappoint their families.

All this experience and learning was eventually put to good use. Gladys has been a teacher, family mediator, librarian, student, business consultant, caterer and food writer. For over 25 years the young bride who could not cook has been an important name in the food industry. She has established and run restaurants, written a book on Indian cooking and developed a deep knowledge of the herbs and spices grown and used in Asian food.

Life as Indians in a time of White Australia was always considered temporary and when the policy changed, the Roach family had to rethink whether they would become Australian citizens. They did, because, as Gladys said, 'Australia offered me everything I believe in; everyone being equal no matter the hierarchy. Australia allowed me to explore different things. I explored more options than I would have if I had lived anywhere else.'

Neville Roach

In 1961 Neville Roach came to Australia from Bombay as a young graduate working with an Indian insurance company. He was based in Adelaide and remembers there were 27 Indians in the whole city, mostly students. He was on a temporary visa and assumed he would return to India. Instead he joined IBM and agreed to work for them for seven years. At the end of that time the White Australia policy had been dismantled and everything had changed – Neville stayed with IBM until 1980. He was the first non-white computer programmer to be given permanent resident status.

Neville quickly became involved in the business and community life of Adelaide. He admired the egalitarian approach of Australians to work and life, and especially the relationship between employer and employee. This suited the behaviour and philosophy of a man who was 'not too respectful of authority' and did not wish to treat his people as inferiors.

In 1989 Neville Roach became managing director of Fujitsu Australia. He has been a significant figure in the growth and development of the computer industry. He has provided Australian leadership in the region in his role as chairman of the Asian Oceanian Computing Industry Organisation, in addition to chairing the Australian Information Industry Association from 1994 through 1996.

Neville Roach has a portfolio of directorships ranging from Fujitsu in Australia, India, New Zealand and Asia to the Special Broadcasting Service. He also chairs the National Multicultural Advisory Council, which reports to the Federal Minister. He has been assertive about his role as a migrant and is a strong role model in the community. He has been consistent in his support of multiculturalism and the power of diversity, and has lobbied to keep it bipartisan. Equally, he has promoted Australia's engagement with the Asian region.

The Roach family has contributed three citizens of whom they are proud and who finally persuaded their parents to become Australian citizens. They have no problem being Indian-Australian or Australian-Indian, except in the cricket season.

'I just could not contemplate that I may have ended up like one of my cousins, picking chestnuts and bearing five children.'

Sarina Russo

Sarina Russo arrived in Australia from Italy, with her mother, at the age of five, to join her father who had emigrated several years earlier. Her father's dream was to have his own vineyard, and he achieved this with the help of his industrious children. Sarina was often the family interpreter, even though she was struggling with English. She recalls negotiating with the Committee of Fruit Marketing and says her father inspired her business acumen from the age of 10. She completed the tax returns and accompanied her father when consulting with his lawyers.

Today Sarina is managing director of one of the largest privately owned educational providers, employing up to 200 full-time and part-time staff and training thousands of Australians and international students each year. The Russo Institute of Technology has facilities in English, Business, Information and Technology, Hospitality and Travel.

It would be easy to forget that this is the achievement of a young woman who was dismissed more than once for her failure to conform as a legal secretary. In 1979 she decided to start her own business and began a typing school with a $2500 overdraft, nine students, rented premises, a part-time commercial teacher and an office junior. The Russo Institute of Technology is today housed in a building called the Sarina Russo Centre. It is a substantial 12-storey building, owned outright by her company. Sarina has recently purchased another Brisbane CBD building which will be refurbished and utilised to accommodate her expanding business, including the future delivery of the second and third years of a degree program in partnership with the University of Southern Queensland.

She made her first return visit to Sicily when she was 28, to see the village that the family had left to create a better life in Australia. 'I just could not contemplate that I may have ended up like one of my cousins, picking chestnuts and bearing five children,' she says. 'It was something for which I had never thanked my father. I immediately phoned him and said, "Dad, I've never thanked you for anything but I've got to thank you for taking me to Australia."'

Miguel Sanz

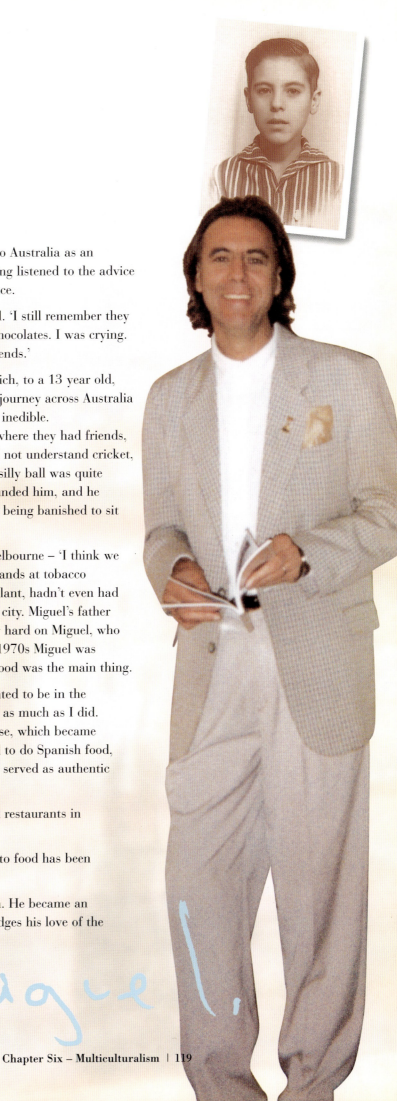

Miguel Sanz was born in Spain and came reluctantly to Australia as an adolescent in 1963. His parents decided to move, having listened to the advice of their friends, who thought Australia was a great place.

'It was the last place I wanted to come to,' says Miguel. 'I still remember they had to push me into the aeroplane. They bought me chocolates. I was crying. I was 13 years of age at that time and I had all my friends.'

The first contact in Perth was a hostel at Northam which, to a 13 year old, was like a concentration camp with lizards. The train journey across Australia was fun except for the food, which the family thought inedible.

For 12 months the Sanz family lived in Port Kembla where they had friends, and Miguel attended school. He had no English, could not understand cricket, and thought the way they played football with a very silly ball was quite extraordinary. The institutionalised sexism also confounded him, and he quickly discovered the joy of a punishment which was being banished to sit with the girls.

Miguel doesn't remember why the family moved to Melbourne – 'I think we just followed some Spanish people'. They tried their hands at tobacco farming, even though they had never seen a tobacco plant, hadn't even had a garden of their own, living, as they did, in the inner city. Miguel's father became a share farmer in tobacco. This was especially hard on Miguel, who didn't go to school as often as he should have. In the 1970s Miguel was involved in the music industry managing bands, but food was the main thing.

'I've always loved food,' he says, 'and I've always wanted to be in the restaurant business. I met my wife and she loved food as much as I did. We opened a little place, The Gourmet Sandwich House, which became a popular spot for Melbourne lunch. But I still wanted to do Spanish food, as I was continually annoyed by the poor quality food served as authentic Spanish.

'We opened Miguel's, and it became one of the top ten restaurants in Melbourne.'

Others followed, and from that time the commitment to food has been constant.

Miguel Sanz thinks of himself as a Spanish-Australian. He became an Australian citizen in the late 1970s but still acknowledges his love of the Spanish way of life.

Joseph Saragossi AO

Joe Saragossi arrived in Australia with the United States army in 1946. An electrical engineer, Lieutenant Saragossi was commanding officer of the Southwest Pacific liaison section, and had charge of all the communications and weather equipment. He was in Australia to close down American operations at Queensland's Amberley Air Force Base, hand it back to the RAAF and effect Eagle Farm's transfer back to civil aviation.

He returned to the United States keen to start an electrical contracting business, but materials were scarce and he decided to try his luck again in Queensland. The GI Bill offered him an opportunity to return to university and finish his degree in electrical engineering. However, after a short time, he chose marriage to Pearle James, an Australian girl he had met as a GI and the daughter of George James, a glass merchant.

Joe started an electrical business in the Queensland town of Beaudesert, where he had unlimited work as the power lines were being installed. He learned about irrigation and milking machinery and loved the life. However when Pearle's father died, the daughters bought out the business and Joe joined the general manager to work at G. James.

He learned about the new business from the ground up and expanded to Toowoomba and other major centres in Queensland, Sydney and Melbourne. As competition in the glass industry grew, the company expanded and diversified into aluminium extrusion, a move which proved very successful.

Joe became a citizen on his 70th birthday, but not before the United States government allowed dual citizenship. On immigration he says: 'I think Australia is utterly crazy not accepting educated migrants. It saves the government millions of dollars in training costs as these migrants are already fully trained and Australia is reaping the rewards.'

Dagmar Schmidmaier

Dagmar Schmidmaier's mother was German, but she grew up in Palestine. She was in Germany as part of her growing up tradition when the war broke out. After the war the opportunity to start all over again in a new country proved very tempting. Dagmar and her mother left Germany as sponsored and assisted migrants and sailed into Sydney Harbour in January 1949. Dagmar's most pressing problem was wondering whether their ship would fit under the Sydney Harbour Bridge.

Now the State Librarian and Chief Executive of the State Library of New South Wales, one of Australia's leading research and information libraries, Dagmar was appointed to this position in 1995.

Dagmar was raised with the assumption that she would attend university and contribute to society. She attended Balgowlah Primary School, where she and her cousin were the only migrant children, and then Narrabeen Girls High, where her Germanic name provided some character-building moments. But she did pretty well in high school – she was on all the sports teams and, in her final year, was house captain and prefect.

Professionally, Dagmar has made a major contribution to Australia. She has been a good and creative teacher and librarian and is an effective role model as both librarian and parent. Her work in the higher education sector, including TAFE and the Colleges of Advanced Education, was recognised by her award of Doctor of Letters (honoris causa) from the University of New South Wales in 1999. Prior to that she had been awarded a Fulbright Scholarship in 1988/89.

The opportunity to pursue whatever ambitions you have and to do that freely is what Dagmar values most about Australia. 'To be able to pass all sorts of boundaries without being unduly aggressive is possible in Australia,' she says. 'It's hard work, but when we go back to Germany – and in England too – the societal structures are so strong and they are so traditionalist. I just don't think there are the same opportunities, particularly for a young woman who had no connections into local social structures.'

Chapter Six – Multiculturalism | 121

Chapter Seven
Immigration

The shift in Australia's post-war thinking and practice in immigration matters revealed how Australia saw itself as part of the new international order. Immigration was included in post-war reconstruction planning, for national development and national survival, population was considered to be vital. Fertility rates were low and immigration seemed a better proposition than raising the birth rates.

Continental Europe was accepted as a source for Australian immigration alongside the United Kingdom. The white alien immigration policy reflected a policy shift which changed Australia forever. Newcomers in that category were considered to be 'givers' rather than the potential 'takers' they had been painted for so long. A target of 70,000 a year was suggested and, in 1948, the target was reached and included 10,000 from refugee camps in Europe.

There was division in the Commonwealth government about accepting refugees but the reality was that not enough people from Continental Europe wanted to come and so the government moved to attract Displaced Persons (DPs). DPs were offered contracts for two years provided they worked where required. In the five years between 1948 and 1952 the average annual intake was around 34,000 despite the initial agreement to average 12,000. This scheme had all but dried up by 1952 but large-scale immigration continued to be promoted on the grounds that it would serve development and enhance Australia's security.

The Australian community was assured that care had been taken with the selection to ensure that those chosen would fit smoothly into our way of life. Assimilation was to be achieved and reception centres would instruct migrants on Australian life, teach basic English and allocate work. Newcomers were advised not to speak their native language in public and to refrain from using their hands in conversation. This was to avoid being conspicuous. To assimilate was to become a 'good' Australian. It aimed at cultural uniformity.

Assimilation was replaced by integration which envisaged a community built on diverse cultural patterns. In the 1960s Aborigines obtained Citizenship and, in the 1970s, the White Australia Policy was abandoned. The people profiled in these chapters arrived post-1949 and were both observers and players in these changes.

While it is probably a reasonable assumption that immigrants will be in favour of immigration, given the diversity of cultural backgrounds and the continual political and community discussion about national immigration policy, asking for their views seemed appropriate. Predictably all could speak enthusiastically about the value of immigration but not all agreed on how many, under what circumstances and from where these immigrants should come.

The significant point of agreement is that immigration is energising and nation-building and, as Australia's population ages, immigration is needed for both economic and creative growth.

Elsa Atkin

I believe our immigration policy should be constantly reviewed to really develop it so that it enhances the future of Australia as well as ensuring that there is a stream of immigration for humanitarian reasons. I think it is really important to have a stream of immigration that is always open for humanitarian reasons. But I also believe that, with a big country like ours, we should hold on to it. I believe we should be able to open it and bring in people who we believe are needed to help this country.

Wolf Blass

I personally don't think we should have an imbalance. An imbalance in a country, I have noticed, makes people very unhappy and unsure of themselves. I have noticed this when I go to Scandinavia, that there is a resentment towards the newly-arrived refugees. This resentment is sitting very deeply in the social psyche particularly since the new arrivals are being supported financially by people who have lived and worked all their lives to make their country great. Now they have to share something with people who have not contributed.

Caroline Baum

I would have to know more about the figures but I am sure we have enough room and enough space and enough of everything to accommodate people who really want to come here and feel they can make a go of it here.

Paul Boyatzis

I think we should have more immigration over the next few years. We need the population. Immigrants do keep us younger in mind and body. If an ethnic underclass is emerging I would think of it as a very temporary situation. I think the descendants of immigrants are upwardly-mobile, in some cases more than others. Certainly from our background I would think the mobility is very much upwardly-mobile but it tends to decrease as the generations increase. Upwards, then a levelling. I totally disagree with the statement that immigration undermines social cohesion and national identity. Immigrants do keep us younger in mind and body.

Les Cassar

I believe immigration creates work. It creates jobs, it creates wealth. I remember when I joined Qantas at the end of school, there were seven companies who were after us. Now kids find it very difficult and I think migration would improve the number of jobs.

Mala Dharmananda

Some of the research strongly suggests immigration is good for the economy. At the same time I'm prepared to concede the environmental and economically sustainable arguments about whether Australia can sustain a bigger population on those grounds alone and I think it goes back to what your criteria for immigration is. Are they family reunions? Are they business migrants who pay a lot of money to come in? On what criteria are we letting people in? Are we going to accept their qualifications? Doctors are a good example. Do we accept their qualifications? We let them in but then they can't practise here. You send them out to country areas and there they can practise for two years without sitting the exams. I'd like to know how these anomalies exist. Australia will accept degrees from universities in Britain, Canada or America, even if they're not in the top league, but won't accept degrees from top universities in India.

Petro Georgiou

I think that immigration levels have to adapt to circumstances. They do have to respond to the needs of the economy. They do have to have a significant humanitarian, non-economic component, but that's only one component. That is my overall view. I do believe in substantial immigration. I think it is important to our national strength, however you care to define it. It seems to me that sometimes the economists, by looking at individual measures, actually miss the point that we are a nation which is greater than GDP divided by population. We are an entity which is larger than the sum of its parts.

Bill Jegorow

I believe it is a matter of populating or perishing. Not only because business, for instance, recognises we are an Asian society, but also it is a stark factor that, in the eyes of many, we are an empty continent. Our environment is fragile, but surely the tremendous damage that has occurred in the past was done by the pastoralists. Surely we have sufficient 'nous' to make sure that, whilst population is increasing, the environment is not damaged.

Diane Grady

I think immigration is terrific for this country and I think we should have a lot more of it. The immigrants I know, and there are some exceptions, have brought incredible energy and spirit and wealth to this country. Not bringing wealth in, but creating it here. I think we should have more skill-based immigration. I think we are missing out on a lot of very talented people who would love to live in Australia and who would bring great things to the country, but it is so hard to get a visa.

Ted Johnson

I'm definitely in favour of increasing immigration. Our society can afford them. There's going to be the needy, there's going to be those dispossessed, there's going to be those seeking political asylum, but there are skills we're going to get that will complement and supplement those unfortunates who don't come ready-made to fill a job somewhere. I'm certainly actively supporting the idea of immigration from a skills point of view. We just don't have all the skills we need.

Vivi Germanos-Koutsounadis

We have been functioning on zero population for the last 15 years. We are not producing naturally so we really have to have immigration if we want to grow. What's the point of bringing in all these doctors, engineers, everybody and then not recognising their qualifications? We are creating unemployment. Also you are creating more social problems, psychological problems, because these people have to find manual cleaning jobs.

Lou Klepac

I think immigration is a fantastic thing. It's like having a pot in which you have a few native Australians and a lot of convicts and Anglo-Saxons and you think this could be better. So you keep throwing in a few Yugoslavs, a few Italians, a few Germans and so on and it is getting better and better. But the soup has got to be Australian. The moment that one of those free people jumps out and wants to be a gherkin, with a gherkin dress and a gherkin religion it is wrong. You have to be part of the soup. You must assimilate.

Ted Kunkel

I think Australia, economically, in terms of its own growth, can support a population far in advance of 17.5 million to 18 million people. Economically I believe that Australia will be a better place. There is a very great benefit to the current tax reforms that makes Australia a better place as an investment destination for people to come here and bring their money. Investment creates jobs. At the end of the day, the Australians we have now need jobs and there is no reason for that unemployment, with the right investment climate, because we have got everything else. We have food, we have water, we have roads, we have space. All we have to do is create the environment for people to invest. We will look after the kids who need jobs. We will look after the immigrants who need jobs as well.

George Lapaine

I support immigration but there are a lot of people who are getting very nervous about the environment. I really think there is an enrichment in immigration and I think it has added a bit of colour. Believe you me, in 1951 Australia was a very drab society. Drab in culture, drab in dressing, drab in architecture, drab in food, drab even in entertainment. I think this influx of people has given Australia a dynamic set of values which it didn't have before.

Dai Le

Australia has 18 million people and the mass concentration of immigration is based in Sydney and Melbourne. If we do increase it we should spread it out to country towns and not bring them all here and put all the burden on areas where there is such high unemployment already. On top of that we've got, in terms of the South-East Asian community, a lot of young people turning to drugs. Drugs are everywhere but seem to be happening more in an area where there is a high concentration of South-East Asian kids where the people haven't got jobs. At this stage we need to solve that problem before we bring in more people from those areas because we just add to the problems.

Mark Leibler

There are short-term issues of timing. You can't just totally open the floodgates and say everyone who wants to come here can come here immediately so there has to be some controls, but I'm very pro-immigration. I don't believe this country can reach its full potential without more immigration. It's true that some may, on a short term basis, consider that this is going to create problems for our welfare if you let people in, but it also creates huge demand and if you have more demand then you have more scope for increasing employment. I must say I've been greatly influenced in this by what I've seen happening in Israel with this huge immigration from the former Soviet Union. Yes, there has been a bit of dislocation, but these people have made a huge contribution to the society that they've settled down in and the country wouldn't be what it is today without immigration.

George Mure

I think it's very good for the country. I think it is Australia's strength. Maybe I am biased but I think it is just great. The fishing industry in particular has benefited enormously from migration. The Italians, the Greeks, the Portuguese to start with, kicked the whole show off. On the other side of it, the Asian market has turned us on to things like abalone, which was known as mutton fish. This is being developed by the Asians and people have come to Australia who understand that.

Satendra Nandan

I think Australia should care a little more for the Pacific. I think it has an obligation to people of Indian origin who were taken there to serve the interests of the CSR company which was Australia's most powerful organisation at that time. To leave them marooned in Fiji ... they should be a little more generous to Fijian Indians. New Zealand was deeply generous and has benefited the most from the coups with 40,000–50,000 Indians, all professional people. If Australia can be a little more generous you would get people who know English, who are very hard working, people with connections, historical and geographical. I think you would be inviting some wonderful citizens to come here and serve.

Juliana Nkrumah

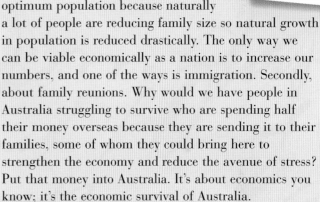

This nation needs to strengthen its immigration policy. It's a big country. I don't understand this thing about optimum population because naturally a lot of people are reducing family size so natural growth in population is reduced drastically. The only way we can be viable economically as a nation is to increase our numbers, and one of the ways is immigration. Secondly, about family reunions. Why would we have people in Australia struggling to survive who are spending half their money overseas because they are sending it to their families, some of whom they could bring here to strengthen the economy and reduce the avenue of stress? Put that money into Australia. It's about economics you know; it's the economic survival of Australia.

Sir Arvi Parbo

There is absolutely no question we must have immigration. We couldn't stay here on a great continent like this in the middle of a sea of overcrowded countries to the north of us and hope to be able to maintain the guardianship of this country with a shrinking population. How could you do that? That would be just not possible. We must have immigration, there is no doubt about it. The only question is, what kind of immigration, and at what rate? Quite clearly I don't think we want to bring people to this country who will then become a burden on the rest of the community. This is not sensible and we can't afford to do it. So we must bring people to this country who are either going to contribute to the community, or bring family members when there is a humanitarian reason for having them. It is silly to say we don't want any immigration; that is like cutting your own throat.

Rolando Ramos

The more immigration the better. It is a big country. I think that migration has always helped countries in many ways all through history. Migration in the beginning was a practical thing to bring workers here. But then it evolved into something different. Migration brings so many skills, so many different points of view, so many contacts with different cultures that it is fantastic. I think there is no way for a country to grow just inside itself. A country needs to grow with the outside world as human beings do. You don't grow just by being by yourself and thinking about yourself and doing things for yourself. The basic way to grow is to meet other people, to share with other people, to exchange points of view, to interact and so on.

Miguel Sanz

I am here and I think I am a very good example of what we've achieved. We have worked very hard and I like to think that we've done things that have certainly benefited this country. But I think we have to be more selective. I think about how it was, to what it is now. You only have to read the paper about drugs and killings. There was an article in the paper that said if you describe a person who has committed a crime you are no longer allowed to say that that person was of Chinese background, or Indian background. But how can you explain that to someone? If I go out and am robbed by a person of a different colour I am going to say it was a black person, or of Greek origin. We all have very different features I think. I wondered what this country had come to. I think if I did something wrong, bad enough, and they wanted to send me back home, I think they should.

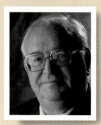

Joe Saragossi

Well I am in the building industry, but every industry you go to where migrants are involved you see the contribution they have made. The Italians did very well here originally on construction and housing. They still do engineering and all sorts of things. The Dutch contributed a lot. The English migrants whinge like bloody hell but they did contribute. The Vietnamese are making a great contribution too.

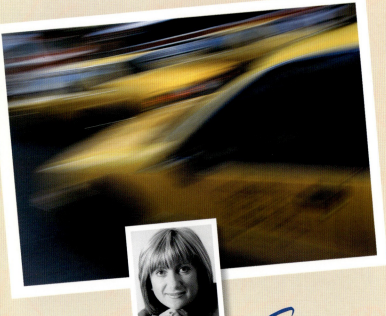

Sarina Russo

I strongly believe that we have to understand that what has made America great is its immigration policy. New York is one of the most exciting cities and it is multicultural. The Jews and the Italians and the Greeks have contributed so much with their energy and commitment to their new country. We can see it on a smaller scale in Australia. The Italians and the Greeks and the Germans, the Chinese, the Japanese, what they have contributed has been fabulous.

Dagmar Schmidmaier

I believe Australia is one of the countries where immigration has worked remarkably well. I do think one needs to take care, and we need to learn from the experiences of other countries around the world. I think, when there are critical issues overseas and wars that cause our environment to reverberate around us, we need to think about how we are affected internally. We need to ensure that those things we all hold so dear are not swept away. We are a wonderful island state so we can, in fact, exert some measure of control which other countries may not be able to do. But I do think an important part of being Australian is to keep the flow of people coming.

Con Sciacca

My personal, not party, view, is that Australia needs a much higher population. We should be thinking about what kind of population we want in 30 years time. Take the long term view; we need a bigger immigration intake to feed more people, to be able to lose our dependency on older people. We need to build an immigration program of younger people. But most importantly we will have to take the community with us. The people who rub shoulders with the new arrivals are the people who need to understand that cultural diversity is best for us.

Jim Spigelman

If our migration had been focused on the traditional composition of society then you would still have a significant range of creative individuals but obviously it wouldn't have been the same. So the difference that has occurred began with the immediate post-war migration and was reinforced over that period, and then in the late 1970s or 1980s, there was significant Asian migration. What you have is a much more diverse and rich community.

Agnes Whiten

Immigration is a very strong force. I came here in 1972 and 27 years later Australia is a vibrant society. This is the only society where you can be yourself. It is not just being able to eat different food. We have multiculturalism. Where else can you have a place that is free? You can be what you are and I think that's the greatest asset. You can be what you are as long as you follow the legal system and the system of government.

Jim Trambas

In Tasmania we need another half a million people. We don't appreciate what we've got here. I brought my brother here. He had a good job back in Greece and I brought him out as a manager. He was in my office recently and he said, 'Jim, the only thing I regret in my life is 20 years ago when you asked me to come here, I didn't come.'

Ngoc Trang Thomas

The mix of immigration is more important than the sheer number. We have to do our duty as a global citizen, giving humanitarian help to those who desperately need it. We have to help family reunion programs. A very important part of the immigration program that is often overlooked is that in many cultures the family has a different meaning. Brothers and sisters are very important; supporting older parents is extremely important. If the children live a prosperous life and can't help their old parents in some way, then they can't live in peace. I think they should be given the choice of bringing their parents here to be looked after, rather than there being just a blanket decision that old people coming to Australia will be a burden to Medicare.

Magda Wollner

From the day whoever made the world said 'get, walk, go' there has been immigration. There is no nation in the world that didn't pinch their land from somebody else. Yes, I am for immigration but it should be people coming here and learning to be an Australian.

The Hon Con Sciacca MP

Con Sciacca was born in Piedimonte Etneo in Sicily in 1947 and arrived in Australia in 1951. His parents, Salvatore and Vincenzina, were only 21 and 23 when they came to Australia where Salvatore began working as a cane cutter in North Queensland. They chose Australia because they had an uncle here who sponsored them.

Con's parents worked hard to educate and provide a better life for their children, and Con's father was variously a share farmer, a hotel owner and manager and an owner of an import/export business. He employed hundreds of people during his working life and his wife worked closely with him.

Con Sciacca graduated in law from the University of Queensland and immediately established his own legal practice. He says he was raised to have a strong sense of social responsibility and became involved in community affairs very early. In 1987 he became a member of the House of Representatives, representing the Federal seat of Bowman. He immediately became Secretary of the Caucus Committee on Immigration, Local Government and Ethnic Affairs. In 1990 he was appointed Parliamentary Secretary to the Minister for Social Security. In 1993 he was given added responsibility as Parliamentary Secretary to the Minister for Arts and Administration.

In March 1994 he was appointed the Minister for Veterans Affairs. In October 1995 he was proud to have been the Minister for the powerful program, *Australia Remembers*. This was an opportunity for him to repay and recognise the life Australia had given him.

He is a strong supporter of cultural diversity and believes Australia does it well. He has a strong personal view that we should encourage much higher levels of immigration, especially of younger people with skills.

'We have over 200 cultures making up Australian culture and helping us move towards an identity of what that is,' he says. 'We can value the culture we left behind while embracing the new and that is a wonderful opportunity.'

He believes that Australia needs a bigger immigration intake to expand our domestic consumer base and minimise the dependence on older people but he also believes that it is important to have mainstream Australians agree.

'The people who rub shoulders with the new arrivals are the people who need to understand that cultural diversity is best for us,' he says.

Fred Shahin

Fred Shahin was born in Palestine and migrated with his family to Lebanon in 1949. He worked for the United Nations in accounting and auditing for 28 years and met many Australians who encouraged his curiosity about the country. When he had to leave Beirut in 1984 because of the war disturbances and his fear for the safety of his family, he had a choice of the United States, Canada and Australia and chose Australia because Australia refused his application on age grounds. He appealed and won. The family chose to settle in South Australia because of its Mediterranean climate.

He and his wife put their $200,000 life savings into a service station and a small house in suburban Adelaide. It was a very successful venture and within five years he, with his sons, brothers and family members, owned three service stations and had developed two Smokemart stores, purchased in 1986, into a retail chain of 40 stores.

Shahin Enterprises which owns Smokemart has won awards for fast growth and is now amongst the top 500 unlisted countries in Australia. Smokemart is now represented in all states of Australia with a total number of 160 stores and has a daily turnover in excess of $1million. This has allowed it to diversify into agriculture, in particular olives and pistachio nuts, and commercial property.

The Shahin family numbers have increased to 70 and are loyal to South Australia and their Islamic heritage. In 1998 the family donated $5 million to build the Islamic Arabic Multicultural Centre in Adelaide. It houses the Al Kahlil Mosque, a library, teaching halls, a home for two priests, and the first Muslim funeral parlour and Muslim cemetery in Australia.

Like most migrants Fred Shahin felt that he became Australian after his first overseas trip. 'When I got back I started talking about how human beings here respect life, how they treat the elderly people, how there is no poverty in Australia and how they feed all these people,' he says.

H Paul Simons AM

At the age of 17 Paul Simons left his native Wales and joined the Merchant Navy as an apprentice deck officer. In 1946 he visited Australia for the first time on a ship carrying a cargo of tea from Ceylon. Whilst in Sydney, he met a young lady, Gwenda Grant, who, in 1952, would become his wife. Their son, David, now a surgeon, was born in 1954 and a daughter, Margaret, an architect, was born in 1958.

Paul had completed his apprenticeship and was 'paid off' his ship, the Ocean Angel in March 1949 at Fremantle. Being a British subject it was possible for Paul to settle in Australia without any formal approval. He joined the Australian Shipping Board (now the National Line) and served with them as a Third Mate on coastal ships until 1953.

In 1954 he joined Woolworths Limited as a management trainee and, after a number of senior appointments, joined the Board as executive director in 1972. From 1974 until December 1978 he acted as joint general manager of the company.

Early in 1979 he was invited by the Hong Kong Dairy Farm company to assist with the acquisition of the Franklins' chain of discount food stores, which was completed in July 1979. He then successfully ran Franklins as CEO until April 1987 when, according to plan, he retired.

Unexpectedly he was invited to return to Woolworths as executive chairman of the Board, which he accepted in May 1987. The company was in decline having suffered a major fall in profits in the preceding year. It was taken over by IEL on May 31 1989 and de-listed. However, the 'Woolies' team rebuilt the business and it was refloated on July 12 1993 in what was then Australia's largest public share offering – one billion shares at $2.45 per share. At his retirement in November 1995 he said 'the highlight of my career was the 1993 float of Woolworths'. The recovery years were not without sadness; Gwenda, his wife of 39 years, died in July 1991 and his longtime friend and CEO, Harry Watts, died in November 1993.

He was remarried to Dr Christine Edwards in June 1994 and, in retirement, they share time between their home in Sydney and their property, Euralie, near Yass, NSW.

Paul became an Australian citizen in 1975 and has received many awards in recognition of his services to business and charity. He was named *BRW*'s Businessman of the Year in 1989 and *Australian Business Monthly*'s Businessman of the Year in 1991.

In that same year he was awarded a Member of the Order of Australia (AM) for services to Australian retailing. In September 1994 he was named Chief Executive Officer of the Year for NSW as a result of a readers' poll conducted by the *Australian Financial Review* newspaper. In November he was named Retailer of the Decade in the *ABM* Top 500 Awards of 1994. In March 1995 Paul Simons received an Honorary Doctorate – in recognition of his 'significant contribution to the retailing industry in Australia' – from Queensland's Griffith University. In November 1995 he was given a special *Bulletin*/Top 500 Award for 'his lifetime contribution to Australian business' – the same month he stepped down as chairman of Woolworths Limited, while remaining as a consultant to the company. In June 1996 Paul Simons was awarded the 1996 Australian Institute of Company Directors' Award for his 'sustained personal contribution to corporate Australia and the wider community'. During 1996–1997 he chaired the committee which reviewed Australia's overseas development aid program. In 1998 he was made an honorary life member of the Spastic Centre of NSW for his charitable work with that organisation.

Commenting on his 50 years in Australia he said: 'I was lucky to have decided in 1949 that Australia would offer more opportunity and a better lifestyle than the UK. The sunshine, the feeling of vitality and the down-to-earth lack of class distinction of the people was such as attractive option to dull war-torn Britain it was irresistible. It has more than fulfilled my wildest dreams and expectations. It's just a pity one must grow old as I feel the best is yet to come for this wonderful, multicultural country.'

Jim Spigelman

The Honourable James Jacob Spigelman QC, Chief Justice of the Supreme Court of New South Wales, was born in Poland in 1946. In 1949 the family had arrived in Australia leaving Poland because, as Polish Jews, the experience of the Holocaust was such that virtually the entire community migrated to the United States, Israel or Australia. There were no relatives to leave as Jewish Poland had ceased to exist.

'I never thought I was Polish,' he says. 'The Poland I came from was Jewish Poland and that had ceased to exist, so I never had an identification of any character with Poland. Nor did my parents. Those that survived the Holocaust, and most hadn't, had left. The community from which they came no longer existed in that place, so, in my case, there was no rival identification.'

The Spigelmans lived in the Sydney suburb of Maroubra and Jim attended Maroubra Bay Public School where there was only one other Jew in the class and two or three other migrants. Sydney Boys High and the University of Sydney followed, with academic success and recognition. Post university he became Senior Adviser and Principal Private Secretary to Gough Whitlam, the then Prime Minister of Australia, positions he occupied from 1972 to 1975. In 1975 he was Secretary of the Department of Media and from 1976 to 1979 a Law Reform Commissioner.

In 1979 he began a successful career at the NSW Bar and was appointed Queen's Counsel in 1986. In 1997 he left private practice to be Acting Solicitor General. In 1998 he was appointed Chief Justice of the Supreme Court of NSW and Lieutenant-Governor of NSW.

Prof Ngoc Trang Thomas AM

Trang Thomas spent her first years in Australia as a student at the University of NSW. She came from Vietnam as a Colombo Plan student and studied Psychology. She chose Australia as she had heard it was a peaceful place. She arrived in Sydney on a windy October day and was assigned to the care of two Salvation Army members, women who ran a small boarding house in Marrickville. She stayed with them for five years and was married from there. Trang learned to be tolerant and accepting, to help others, to give and to share from life in that household. These are among what she calls the best Australian values. Meanwhile, despite her struggles with English, she graduated with First Class Honours in Psychology and was the first Vietnamese to do so.

Trang married David Thomas in 1969 and enrolled in a Masters degree at Macquarie University which she completed in 13 months. After their two daughters were born, she stayed at home for a couple of years and then worked casually as a tutor at the Royal Melbourne Institute of Technology (RMIT). In common with many immigrants, and particularly those from Vietnam, news of the war and loss of family made life painful and that was exacerbated when members of her family were refused entry to Australia and instead emigrated to the United States.

She decided to study again and enrolled as a PhD student at La Trobe, studying older people. Upon receiving that degree and a subsequent research career, she was appointed the first female professor at RMIT and in 1993 she was appointed the first woman chair of the Victorian Ethnic Affairs Commission, a post she held until 1997. The *Melbourne Age* described Trang Thomas as 'one of the calmest ethnic community voices and a great believer in Australia's record of tolerance'.

She serves the Australian community in many ways. She is a director of SBS, a member of the National Council for the Centenary of Federation, a board member of the Council of Adult Education and is a constant voice in the debate on multiculturalism.

'I hope Australians of various heritages will treasure and maintain their culture in Australia but also feel detached enough to view actions of "old" countries with dispassionate eyes,' she says.

Chapter Eight
Individual Contribution

Asking people to describe their contribution to Australia is quite confronting, rather like asking them to write their own obituary. Those of us who have been here for a couple of generations have probably not thought about it. I wondered if new arrivals had. It was clear to me, when selecting people to be interviewed, that all the interviewees had made a mark on Australia. Could they see it, and how much had they thought about it?

What motivated it? Did their relationship with their new home provoke a response of gratitude and a need to give something back? Did they feel the need to move beyond survival if they had come from a politically repressive regime? Were the individual migrants people who would seize and or create opportunities in any environment?

The responses suggest all of the above and more, and leadership emerges as a common theme. This often begins within their own communities, but invariably reaches into the wider community. There are examples of leadership in social and community issues, business, politics, the arts and agriculture. Seemingly quintessential Australian pursuits have had value added to them and somehow they have become more, rather than less, Australian. Perhaps the concept of being Australian has changed.

We have learned new ways to be Australian from our new citizens. They have encouraged us to value our way of life and not take it for granted. When we listen to their voices, we have an opportunity to see our immediate world with new eyes and re-think what it means to be Australian.

The range of contributions these Australians have made is breathtaking. They have footprinted Australian life, and without their contribution, our present culture would be unrecognisable. They confirm our status as an immigrant culture.

Caroline Baum

I just want to be allowed to participate in the debate on an equal footing with everybody else. If I am able to do that, if I am able to feel that I am contributing by being engaged in cultural discussion, by being able to be a member of the media and the artistic life of the community, then I will feel very satisfied and very privileged. I have become so passionate about Australian literature and Australian writing, and it has been a fantastic time to be passionate about it because it has flourished in so many incarnations. To have been able to work in parallel with that flourishing has been an absolute joy.

Tim Besley

The single best contribution to Australia – well, probably one of the most interesting ones – was the very close involvement I've had as the Commonwealth Bank has gone from wholly government ownership to wholly private ownership, with all the attendant discussions, sometimes full and frank, with ministers and so on. That has been good fun.

Paul Boyatzis

My family, I would say. What is wealth? I define wealth in terms of the word 'filotimo'. I would say one has worked, one has provided services here and there, one has joined clubs, one has joined associations – we all have. But contribution, I would think, without sounding too corny, is being able to see three adults, wife of course, happy wife, and a close home environment similar to what one was used to as a child, both in my case and in my wife's case.

Les Cassar

My contribution is that we employ 700 people. My contribution is that my company is as happy an environment as you can get. The integrity of the business adds value. We are selling tickets and people are putting their faith in a dream of a holiday. The integrity of our company is that we give value.

Wolf Blass

I think I was responsible for changing the total wine industry. Why I say that, drinkability is the key word which I personally think I can be hailed for. I have changed the whole wine industry; they all followed me. Initially they couldn't believe that you could drink a young wine, for example, that you can mature wines faster, that you can bring them earlier onto the market, that you need less time and capital involvement. I personally think that whatever I did 20 years ago, Australia and most modern new world wine countries are doing today.

Arlene Chai

My contribution to Australia is offering a different point of view, because of my work. I tend to tell stories about the culture I grew up with. You never walk away from that, and hopefully that shows that regardless of race, the things that drive us are actually the same. We have the same fears as well, and that doesn't change from culture to culture. Those things are fairly common. You won't see so much the difference as the things we have in common.

Mala Dharmananda

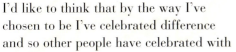

I'd like to think that by the way I've chosen to be I've celebrated difference and so other people have celebrated with me. It's personal and local. It's the woman up the street who might celebrate something with me, might celebrate my daughter's first birthday because that's a big deal in India and we pray and we celebrate. Celebrating in a different way. That's a good way of being – it's less threatening, and I don't mean it in a big professional sense or the public sense. I mean it in the simplest sense, so that a child can come to my house and eat Indian food or wear Indian costumes.

Sir James Gobbo

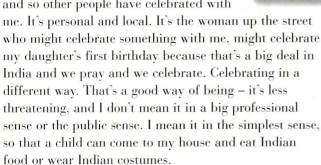

I think what we are seeing is 'fair go' writ large, and if I can be a method of encouragement to others, and there are many like myself who are offering some kind of example of what can be done, then it all helps to preserve this working image of an Australia which is true to its ideals. It is truly a country which is egalitarian and yet prizes success and encourages people to succeed. All of that, I think, is important to convey to the fresh waves of migrants who are coming through the system. It is no good having dreams if dreams don't come true occasionally.

Diane Grady

I suppose I'm doing my best on a number of fronts: helping women become more successful in business; helping organisations do a far better job in helping their employees realise their potential. I think the way work has been structured in many Australian organisations has meant people are not being encouraged or, in some cases, not being allowed to make their form of contribution, so I work to try to change that.

Elena Kats-Chernin

My only contribution to Australia can be my music, and I just think that if I write good enough music, and hopefully I do, and I try to give my best any time I write anything, I think that is my contribution. I do give lectures sometimes, but I don't think that's as good. I do like to talk to students, but that's a very small contribution. I can't do much more. I get very nervous at a performance, especially outside Australia, because you represent Australia in some way. If there are four composers and one of them is you and you're Australian, you don't want to sound bad, because they will think Australian music is not good.

Akira Isogawa

Well I guess, and maybe it is arrogant of me to say, but my creativity. It has been so fortunate that I am doing what I like doing, which is expressing my creativity, and it is being appreciated by a number of Australians. That is what I can offer.

Ted Johnson

I'd like to be able to say that I've done good work in business. I have been very pleased and very motivated by my four years at the RACV. I think I am doing worthwhile things to improve its position and its contribution to the community. I'm actively involved in the Australia–Ireland fund, a group of people in Australia who are gathering funds to contribute to some of the more painful issues of Northern Ireland.

Judit Korner

In some way I have made people aware of skin care: it's not just something frivolous, it's something important which has proved to be so right with the number of melanomas that are growing in Australia. The statistics on that far outweigh other countries. I suppose I've created careers for people who have gone through our schools. But Australia was the country that did it all for me; if I'm clapping, which hand makes the noise, my left or my right? Together it works, don't you think?

Vivi Germanos-Koutsounadis

I think my greatest contribution has been that I have participated in the movement to try to get justice for migrant people, to create the awareness that we are all migrants and we all have common causes and problems but differences as well. Celebrate our differences, work together on our common issues. I really feel privileged to have participated in the Aboriginal issue as well. Because I lived in Redfern and because I worked in Redfern for a long time, I was privileged to participate in the Aboriginal movement. I think multiculturalism was instrumental in creating their awareness, because through multiculturalism we helped the government recognise the disadvantages, the lack of access, the lack of participation, the lack of acknowledgment of the culture and languages of Aboriginal people.

Tan Le

I think the greatest contribution is commitment to the country, and I think my greatest contribution is that I do feel a sense of belonging. I feel committed and I feel passionately about Australia. I don't believe that the future of Australia necessarily has to be the present. It doesn't have to be a continuation of the present. It's what we make of it. And our future is as good as our vision for it. I think the greatest contribution is to believe in it and to have faith in it and to demand that it's a society that's just and fair. I think that's how I'd like to see the country – to be a hopeful country.

Mark Leibler

I think my parents would have said that their major contribution to Australia was leadership and enhancement of Jewish life in this country. But doing so not within a ghetto, but in what's really called a multicultural society which involves a lot of interaction outside the Jewish community as well.

Dai Le

I think I would like to be able to act as a bridge between the Vietnamese people and the wider Australian society. To understand a bit more, understand our plight, understand our journey, why we chose to come to Australia, what were the reasons. I think that is missing. I think while the war played a very important part, because there was a lot of social activism during the war, with students protesting against the war, somehow I don't know whether or not people remember. They know the war happened, but in terms of the people, people like myself who escaped – and there are worse stories than mine – their stories haven't been told. I would love to tell some of those stories so that you can understand me a bit more and I can alleviate your fears about this increased number of Asians in Australia.

Nelson Leong

I think I owe Australia an awful lot. Australia gave me life. Australia gave me opportunity. Australia gave me a lot of freedom. If there is anything I can contribute to this country, I will do it. I don't have any particular thing that I would pick, because I owe Australia a lot. So anything I can contribute to the country, then I will be there.

Satendra Nandan

I think in my teaching I have opened the world of post-colonial studies, which is very important here – putting Australia at the heart as a post-colonial society rather than a colonial European society. It is what I would describe as the opening of the Australian imagination to its geographical position, to its cultural possibilities. Which other country offers this possibility? America doesn't have that; Canada doesn't. We have it. We have the Pacific, we have Asia and we have the European countries. The trinity of these cultures can be the most exciting synthesis for the future. So I think my contribution is in education.

Rolando Ramos

I think that through my profession my contribution has been in bringing, not necessarily my cultural background, because I don't have a traditional sort of dance, my way of thinking that has been influenced maybe by Chile, by my country, maybe my way of analysing things and so on. Maybe some theatrical styles as well: how to direct and so on. I think the biggest contribution of anyone who comes from outside a country is that you can bring different perspectives. You bring different perspectives and therefore you can make the perspective inside people bigger, broader.

Miguel Sanz

Apart from an understanding of the Spanish community, we put a lot of time and effort into that, I think food. We certainly worked very, very hard to change the misconception that people had about food. The days when you put a plate of food in front of someone and they used to lift it up and say, 'What's that muck underneath it?' Or, 'Olives? Haven't you got any radishes?' 'This blue cheese, what is this?' All those things. So yes, that is one area that I have put a lot of time and effort into.

Dagmar Schmidmaier

In my own little way I think I have been a really good teacher and a creative librarian. So professionally I think I have made a contribution, and I will continue to do that. In terms of our kids, I hope what we are able to do is make them really good, tolerant citizens who contribute to society. To give them an attitude that they actually have responsibilities, and it is not just a matter of taking. I think that is an issue with a lot of people today; they talk about their rights but they don't talk a lot about their responsibilities, and I think it is important that they do that.

Fred Shahin

I have been able to create business and an activity to employ over 700 people in Australia, and I have been able to contribute to the Muslim community of Australia by giving them something which will help them settle better in Australia – The Islamic Arabic Centre – at a cost of $5 million. It is a place for worshipping for about 7000 people, a library to link with the culture, teaching halls for lectures to Australians as well as Muslims, a home for two priests and the first Muslim Cemetery in Australia, and the first Muslim funeral parlour in Australia.

Kostya Tszyu

One thing that is very important for me is to get kids to stay away from big trouble. I have tried to create a boxing gym, I have tried to be a boxing trainer. This is my goal. If I get somebody who will become a world champion in the future, that is a great thing. To do something different might be wrong for the community, in my opinion. If you know something you have to give it back, you have to teach these things to people. Boxing is very limited here, and if people don't know, how can you judge them? How can you say, 'You are doing it wrong.' They say, 'Yes I am doing it wrong, but who taught me? Nobody taught me.' I have to teach the young kids. It is not only fighting, it is respect for your opponent, respect for everybody, respect for those older than you.

Ngoc Trang Thomas

I think one thing that I enjoy doing now is providing a role model for the young women, the young migrants. I enjoy very much going out to schools with a high percentage of migrant kids and especially the ones who are about 14 or 15. They often feel very depressed because they feel they have no prospect of making a good life in Australia. I often say to them, when I came to Australia my English was worse than yours. You are young, you'll pick English up in no time. Especially to girls, I always say to them, you can have your career, have your children, as long as you are not too greedy and want everything at once. One thing at a time.

Jim Trambas

I always believe that when I get older I don't have to turn my head back and say, 'did I do enough?' I am very satisfied I did as much as I could for the time I have been here. We have trained a lot of apprentices and helped people here and there.

Wilson Wu

Well I have tried very hard to build bridges between Australia and Malaysia for business. I have tried really hard to encourage my friends in Australia to get to know Asia better. To get rid of misconceptions also about Australia. It works both ways. I have encouraged our children to continue their friendships in Malaysia and here. I would like to add that I am the Acting President of the West Australian Chamber of Commerce and Chair of the Business Council of Western Australia. And I say to all new arrivals, I want to encourage new migrants, they can do it, give back to the community that they are part of. Join organisations. Become part of Australian life.

Agnes Whiten

I think my major contribution to Australia is in my work in the ethnic area as a whole, and pioneering the role of women's advisor to the Archbishop. It was a really wonderful position because I came in as an outsider to a different structure. Even with a good community background, with a good education, they have a different culture. Even the feminist theologians are different from you and me as feminists. They don't relate outside, whereas someone like me does.

Josef Chromy

I have done extremely well for myself in Australia, and I think I have done good for Australia too. I started a little business, a little butcher's shop, and then that grew until I had 18 butcher's shops. I started to make smallgoods in Burnie, Tasmania, and then in Hobart and Launceston. Then there were about seven smallgoods manufacturers and I kept growing. There were about seven meat exporters and I started to export. The businesses grew and grew and finally I ended with 500 people working for me with a $75 million turnover.

Sir Arvi Parbo

I don't know what my contribution has been, but I know what Australia has done for me. It has been really marvellous. I think for a person like me to come here from nowhere with nothing and have all the opportunities to establish yourself and your life and live it the way you want to live it and do what you want to do, work with people you respect and like as I have done all my working life, has really been of great personal satisfaction for me. I hope, in the course of it, I have been able to contribute something to the country.

Neville Roach

I think I've contributed a great deal to the development of our industry and to attitudes in terms of that development in relation to Asia. There is an Asia–Oceania Computing Industry Organisation which Australia and New Zealand are part of. It is purely with Asia, and it is a model that I think Australia should look at for almost all of its relationships.

Gladys Roach

I think because Australia has allowed me to explore different things, I have been able to do different things. Being in Australia forced me to work and I had to do that with limited talent, limited experience, limited qualifications. I explored many more options than I would have if I had lived anywhere else, especially in India. I needed to earn money in the beginning and therefore I did most things, from cleaning to teaching. I taught and I did catering and wrote a couple of books. Things I would never have done.

'There is so mych equity; where the differential between wealthy and workers is not so much.'

Jim Trambas

Jim Trambas was born in Greece, near Salonika. Fresh out of National Service, he was helping a stranger find the West German Embassy by asking a local cop who had been on the beat only two days and who only knew where the Australian Consulate was. Jim recalled that the first floor display had pictures of people on beaches and people in factories wearing white helmets, gloves and glasses. It looked so clean and friendly and he asked what qualifications he would need to go there. The receptionist suggested relatives, a wife or a fiancee. Since he had none of these, he started to leave when she mentioned that if he had finished his matriculation in Greece he could go as a student. Although he had only a smattering of English, he felt confident that he would quickly acquire it.

He arrived in Sydney in 1965 by himself. He was 22 years old, excited and apprehensive. With a couple of friends he headed for Kings Cross and wondered if he was in America, because everything seemed so prosperous. He noticed a little wooden box next to the Greek newspapers where people left their money, and marvelled at the assumed honesty. Then he saw two old men eating out of a rubbish bin. 'I didn't think this happened in Sydney,' he says.

After three months working in Port Kembla and Sydney, the company he was working with transferred him to Gladstone in Queensland. It was an Italian company, working on what was then the biggest job in the southern hemisphere, building Gladstone Aluminium. Eventually, with the same company, he moved to Tasmania.

In 1968 Jim Trambas became an Australian citizen and felt proud to belong to a country 'where there is so much equity; where the differential between wealthy and workers is not so much'. Marrying an Australian confirmed this.

In 1969 he formed Doric Engineering, and the product range was progressively developed until now it manufactures shipping containers, not only fulfilling the demands of the Australian market but exporting 30 to 40 per cent of its product. Jim has recently been asked to supply a specially built machine to make all the components for the roof of the new airport in Athens.

'Next time we go to Athens we can look up at the roof and know we made that in Australia,' he says. 'That is very satisfying.'

Chapter Eight – Individual Contribution | 145

Kostya Tszyu

Kostya Tszyu was born in Serov, Russia, in 1969, and he started boxing at the age of nine. He was six times Russian champion, three times European champion, twice voted most outstanding boxer at the European titles, the 1990 Gold Medallist at the Goodwill Games in Seattle and the 1991 Gold Medallist at the World championships in Sydney.

Kostya arrived in Australia with his then fiancée, Natasha, on January 10 1992 with $1000, one suitcase and no English. This was the beginning of his professional career. Since then he has fought on 24 occasions for 22 wins, 18 of which have come by a way of knockout.

Kostya's only loss in amateur/pro ranks since 1989 was to Vince Phillips in June 1997. His return to the ring was a grand performance and executed in a devastating fashion. In his very next outing, in 1997 in Townsville, he despatched the very highly regarded Ismael Chaves of Argentina inside of three rounds in an official WBC Super Lightweight elimination bout.

On April 5 1998 Kostya was matched against the former World Champion, Calvin Grove, a match that ended in a one-round KO. Kostya contested the final WBC elimination bout against another former World Champion, Rafael Ruelas, in El Paso on August 15, 1998 which resulted in a sensational ninth round knockout.

Kostya was scheduled to fight the number one ranked WBC Super Lightweight contender, Miguel Angle Gonzales, on November 28 1998. However Gonzales suffered a rib injury with only eight days left before the bout. In Gonzales' absence, the highest-ranked available contender was Cuban Champion and Team Freedom Member, Diobelys Hutatdo.

In 1998 Kostya reached the pinnacle of his professional career by becoming the new WBC Super Lightweight World Champion. Now the two-time World Boxing Champion is back to being considered one of the world's best pound-for-pound fighters.

Kostya and Natasha were married in 1993 and have a 4-year-old son Timophey. Natasha gave birth to their

second son, Nikita, on January 19 1998. They live at Sans Souci, Sydney, and have been joined by Kostya's parents and his sister and her family.

Kostya became Australia's own in 1996 when he was the proud recipient of Australian Citizenship. He was twice voted the Sports Star of the Year for the Sutherland Shire and St George area.

'My career as a sportsman is going to finish in a couple of years,' he says. 'What exactly am I going to do? I am going to stay in this area, where I have opened a gym for kids to keep them busy. Troubled kids can come to the gym and I can help by telling them what is wrong and what is right. I can give a different thing to the community. Boxing is very limited here and I have to teach young kids that it is a strong discipline, a very strong discipline.'

Agnes Whiten

Agnes Whiten has the distinction of being the first Women's Adviser to the Catholic Archbishop of Brisbane, a position she held from 1993 to 1996. The position was the first and only one in Australia, and possibly unique in the whole world. She is currently in her third term as a member of the University of Queensland Senate (the first immigrant woman to be elected to this body) and has been reappointed to the National Multicultural Advisory Council. Her other memberships include: Ministerial Advisory Committee for Queensland Women; Board of the National Foundation for Australian Women; National Advisory Committee of Women's Health Australia; Australian Federation of University Women (Qld); Executive of the National Council for Women (Qld); and Executive of the Ethnic Communities Council of Queensland.

Agnes was one of the first women to graduate in metallurgical engineering from the University of the Philippines, in 1964. She was also the first to finish a Master of Science (Met) from the University of the Philippines' Engineering Graduate School. Her first job was at Acoje Mines, a metallurgical chromite mine in the Zambale Ranges.

In 1971 she attended a Mineral Symposium, held at the University of Queensland, where she was the only woman delegate. At the Symposium, she met Dr Bill Whiten, Principal Research Fellow at the Julius Kruttschnitt Mineral Research Centre (JKMRC), whom she later married. Agnes came to Brisbane in 1972 and became the first woman to join the research staff of the JKMRC. She worked there until the birth of her first child in 1981.

It was the birth of her sons that ended her ambivalence about becoming an Australian citizen. 'I wouldn't become an Australian if I was feeling ambivalent,' she says. 'It wasn't fair to Australians and it wasn't fair to my country. When I became an Australian, I took off with my community work. I started with the Filipino community. I wanted to raise the profile of Filipino women and get away from the assumption that we were all mail-order brides.' She is founding president of the Filipino Community Coordinating Council of Queensland, the umbrella body of Filipino-Australian organisations in the State. She is the author of the book, *History of the PASQ Inc.* the Philippine–Australian Society of Queensland, which is the first Filipino association in the State.

Agnes is one of the recipients of the Manila East (V.Mapa) High School Alumni Blue Falcon Award for Community Service for Migrant Filipinos, in connection with the 75th Anniversary of the school in 1998. It is the first time that the recipient of this award was an overseas Filipino – it was given in recognition of her work in Australia.

Chapter Eight – Individual Contribution | 149

Magda Wollner

Magda Wollner came to Australia in 1949 with her husband Igor. Like many immigrants, the decision to choose Australia was almost accidental. Magda was born in Budapest, but she and Igor were Slovaks who met in London, where they had gone in 1939 because of the war. They spent most of the war years in Scotland, where she was happy and he dreamed of living in a sunny place like Jamaica.

They agreed to pursue the Jamaican option and Magda was in the Strand in London looking for the place to make the booking when she met an Australian who advised her to choose Australia instead. She recalls that he said, 'The streets are not paved with gold, but if you want to work hard you will make a future.' They both had British passports and decided Australia was the place. They arrived in Melbourne and both found work. However, after 18 months Igor announced that the weather in Melbourne was too like Glasgow, and Brisbane was where he wanted to be.

In 1950 Igor and Magda settled in Brisbane and Magda decided to open a restaurant. Her working life in the UK had, of necessity, been domestic, and she had worked in private homes in London, and as a manageress in the Czechoslovak-Scottish Club in Glasgow. They bought a place called The Green Door in Queen Street and converted it into the Old Vienna, where they offered traditional European food and ambience. Initially Magda hated Brisbane, but through the restaurant she met people whom she came to love. Her clientele were Australians who desperately wanted to know something about Europe. The Wollners gave Brisbane a place to be European, a place to explore different ideas. They encouraged young artists by hanging their work and introducing them to prospective buyers. They offered a new dimension to the cultural life of Brisbane.

150 | A Fair Go – Portraits of the Australian Dream

Wilson Wu

Born in 1946 to Malaysian parents of Chinese background, Wilson Wu completed his secondary education in 1965 and entered the banking profession as a clerk/teller with the Chartered Bank. By 1973 he had worked his way to Branch Manager level. Meanwhile, studying by correspondence, he obtained the full banking diploma from the Chartered Institute of Bankers (UK) in 1969. Having completed this professional banking qualification, he set about obtaining an external Honours Law degree in 1974 from the University of London, again by self-study through correspondence. One year later, in 1975, the bank sent him to London to study for his Barrister-At-Law degree at Lincoln's Inn.

Returning home, he practised law until 1981, when he left to work in Hong Kong as a corporate lawyer for a large investment company which had business interests in the United Kingdom, Canada, the United States and China. In 1987, when his son David was ten years old, he decided, with his wife, Patricia, to migrate to Perth – they had been there on five previous occasions for family holidays.

Missing his banking environment, Wilson decided to return to financial services and joined Citibank in Perth as an Area Manager, where he again worked his way up to be Vice-President, Western Australia. Today Wilson is Head of Citibank's Retail Bank in Western Australia.

His past community activities include: Chairman, International Business Council of Western Australia; President, Malaysia–Singapore Association; Vice-President, Chung Wah Association; Vice-Chairman, Australia–Indonesia Business Council (WA); President, Hong Kong–Australia Business Association (WA).

Wilson is a very strong believer in giving back to the community that nurtures and supports him and his family. As a proud Australian citizen, he is extremely active in supporting all activities that help create harmony in the community as well as promoting Australia's business interests abroad. This is reflected in his giving all his extra time and energy to support community activities. He is presently the chairman and vice-president of the WA Chinese Chamber Small Business Division.

'Today, for many in Australia, migrants have always been part of the scenery; it's a generational thing. Now, when you observe children in school, most are oblivious to cultural differences. It has come to reflect and embrace some of the best characteristics of what Australia is today.'
—Petro Georgiou MP

Chapter Nine
Australian Multiculturalism
The Strength of Our Diversity

On the eve of the year 2000, Australia's population is made up of its original inhabitants, the Aboriginal people, and an extraordinary combination of the descendants of convicts, free settlers, migrants and refugees who come from nearly 200 countries.

Statistics show that four in 10 Australians are migrants or the children of migrants.

In fact, it could be said that everyone living in Australia, who is not an Aborigine, is a migrant, or has ancestry belonging to another place and another culture which did not originate in Australia.

We are fewer than 20 million and we are evolving with a visible need to understand, include and cherish our differences. From an essentially monocultural and monolingual nation which pursued a White Australia policy, Australia has metamorphosed into a multicultural and multi-lingual country, creating its very own distinctive identity.

From a nation which advocated cultural assimilation, while relegating newcomers to structural separatism, Australia is now committed to cultural pluralism and integration. Our migrants have come from the United Kingdom, Eastern and Western Europe, the Mediterranean, the Middle East, Asia, the Americas, Africa and the Pacific region.

As our national portrait expanded to include all races and religions, so Australian attitudes have changed. Acceptance has moved beyond exotic foods and flavours and folkloric displays to a genuine recognition that the preservation of different cultures and languages represents a national asset.

Bilingualism and biculturalism are no longer seen as threatening national cohesion or precluding national loyalty. Instead, in a global world, they are seen as providing us with the capacity for worldwide political and trade links.

Living and working and playing together are many who, in their former homeland, would have remained fossilised antagonists. The Fair Go philosophy seems to overcome those antagonisms and help them follow different dreams.

There are those who sought to escape poverty and embarked on the voyage to a land which promised, and delivered, opportunities, employment, education, a better life and – what most could not have anticipated – an extraordinary upward social mobility.

The Australian media reflects a diversity of ethnic origins, the trade union movement is led by an overseas-born woman, and many significant political party strategists are either overseas born or descended from non-English-speaking migrants. Many of Australia's top corporate executives, diplomats, lawyers, doctors and academics have names indicating a wide diversity in their genealogical lineage.

The tycoons of industry, real estate developers and business generally indicate the same diversity. And *Business Review Weekly*'s annual list of the country's richest reveals that their achievements have been financially rewarded.

According to the Australian Bureau of Statistics and the Department of Immigration and Multicultural Affairs, Australia's population may reach between 23.5 million and 26.4 million by the year 2051.
It is unlikely, on present fertility rates, that this can be achieved without significant immigration.

The sources of our future migrants may have a powerful impact on our society. Looking back on the last 50 years, and the changes which have emerged following immigration, we can only be excited at the prospect of growth and diversity. We have evolved from a Eurocentric colonial nation to an inclusive multicultural society with a promising future. We have become like our own opal – many colours within one resplendent stone. —Isabel Lukas

Isabel Lukas arrived in Sydney from Argentina in 1966 with no English. Less than a decade later she pioneered coverage of ethnic affairs on Australia's oldest newspaper, *The Sydney Morning Herald*. Born in Buenos Aires to post-World War II Polish refugees, she was raised bilingual – Spanish and Polish – and bicultural. When the family migrated to Australia in search of better opportunities and democracy she was almost 16, and determined to become a journalist. Isabel learned English by reading *Time* magazine with the aid of a dictionary. 'It never occurred to me that because English was not my mother tongue – in fact it would be my third language – that it would be an impediment to becoming a journalist,' she says. 'I applied for a cadetship to the newspapers that I thought were respectable: *The Australian*, *The Financial Review* and *The Sydney Morning Herald*. I managed to persuade the *Herald* to select me. I became the first editorial cadet of non-English speaking background.'

Chapter Nine – The Strength of Our Diversity

The Strength of Our Diversity

Australia is, and always will be, a multicultural society, regardless of our future migrant intake. Our Indigenous people have always had a rich variety of cultures, languages and customs, although our early settlers were, for the most part, unable to recognise that diversity. Indeed, our early settlers were diverse, whether they were members of the First Fleet or Japanese pearlers in north Western Australia or Portuguese or Spanish missionaries on the Western Australian coast. The use of indentured labour in Queensland, and the arrival of 40,000 Chinese on the goldfields of Victoria in the 19th century, added to that diversity. Today, it continues to grow.

Over the last 50 years our diversity has grown rapidly as a result of the large-scale migration programs encouraged by governments, irrespective of party politics. The shift of policy, from a White Australia to a non-discriminatory migration policy, was a giant leap in public policy and failed to fulfil the doomsayers' predictions of social upheaval. The existing Australian population demonstrated its expansive ability to accommodate newcomers and settle them in. Now Australia is one of the world's leaders in managing cultural diversity.

PUBLIC POLICY

How the newcomers were settled in has also changed. Public policy moved from assimilation to integration and then to multiculturalism, the logical development of that process. With increased globalisation, which had its roots in the mass movement of people in the decades following World War II, governments recognised the need for a positive policy to manage cultural diversity effectively. Started in Australia by Labor Prime Minister Gough Whitlam and then consolidated by the Liberal government of Prime Minister Malcolm Fraser, multiculturalism was developed to manage cultural diversity without conflict. The establishment of Ethnic Community Councils, both nationally and in various States, provided leadership and new relationships for the voices of diversity.

Assimilation was based on a belief in the benefits of homogeneity and a shared vision of a white society. It excluded non-European immigration and had a profound impact on our Indigenous people, who could neither accept nor conform to a white image. Integration, which envisaged a community built on diverse cultural patterns, found a ready place among the strands of thought about pluralism after World War II. However, in the early 1970s, integration as public policy gave way to multiculturalism.

It was the New South Wales government which first recognised that a culturally diverse society would require different approaches in creating social policies. Although this was probably an evolutionary process that began the day the first fleet arrived in Sydney Harbour, real change could not occur until there were formal decisions by government and the implementation of necessary policies. That began with the passing in 1976 of the Ethnic Affairs Bill by the New South Wales government which recognised the need for governments to tailor services to meet the specific needs of ethnic communities.

When the Federal Government established the Australian Institute of Multicultural Affairs in Melbourne in 1979, with Petro Georgiou as its director, it confirmed multiculturalism as the official public policy and philosophy. The Office of Multicultural Affairs was established in March 1987 in the Department of Prime Minister and Cabinet and in July 1989 it published *The National Agenda for a Multicultural Australia*. This landmark document set the tone nationally for multicultural policy and continues to have bipartisan political support.

Multiculturalism recognises and accepts that Australia is a culturally diverse and inclusive country where social harmony is promoted and where everyone in the community has to make some adjustments. The newcomer has an obligation to accept the basic structure of Australian society – the Constitution and the rule of law and English as the national language. In return, Australia must make migrants feel welcome and ensure that equal opportunity includes them. Australian multiculturalism appreciates that many migrants will choose to retain some of their cultural heritage of particular customs and traditions. Often these will be adopted by other Australians. We must all feel free to choose which customs or traditions we retain, or adopt, within the framework of our legal democracy.

> How do you make public policy work better? Multiculturalism is probably the greatest challenge facing western democracies into the next century. How do you make people from diverse backgrounds relate with a core of shared values so that they can get on, feel at home with each other, and be productive for the country?
> —Jason Yat-sen Li, lawyer.

CITIZENSHIP

Australia celebrated 50 years of Citizenship in 1999. When the Nationality and Citizenship Act of 1948 came into force on January 26, 1949, Citizenship became a legal reality. Commenting on the first nationwide naturalisations, the Department of Immigration boasted, in its 1950 publication, *They Became Australian Citizens*: 'It is a proud day for Australia, for another person has expressed so complete a faith in this country that he is prepared to put it before all others, even the land of his birth.'

While an Australian citizen remained a British subject, Australian Citizenship laws gradually became more inclusive, with barriers progressively removed. Today the Citizenship Pledge asks that new citizens pledge their loyalty to Australia and its people and promise to share their democratic beliefs, respect their rights and liberties, and uphold and obey the laws of Australia.

Australian Citizenship has been a unifying process in the development of Australian nationhood and Australian multiculturalism. It is often the threshold moment, when people feel they can identify as Australians and take an active part

Chapter Nine – The Strength of Our Diversity

in the affairs of the nation. Citizenship requires a clear commitment to Australia's national interests, while recognising and respecting diversity. It helps us focus on the concept of inclusiveness.

> We are often told that modern Australia was born out of a deeply racist experience and that a defining dynamic of our society today is a process of freeing ourselves from this bigoted and reactionary legacy.
> — Stepan Kerkyasharian AM,
> Chairman of the Ethnic Affairs Commission of New South Wales.

MULTICULTURALISM

Australian multiculturalism asks that all Australians fulfil their civic duty by observing the fundamentals of Australian society – our constitution, our democratic institutions and our values. It also respects, subject to the law, the right to express one's own culture and beliefs and involves a reciprocal obligation to accept the right of others to do the same. The principle of social equity, which assumes an entitlement to equality of treatment and opportunity for all Australians to contribute to the social, political and economic life of Australia, free from discrimination, is another unifying thread in Australian multiculturalism.

Recently analysts and commentators have promoted the concept of productive diversity. This notion sees the diversity of skills and abilities available through multiculturalism as an investment in the national interest, something which produces dividends for the whole Australian community. In a world where technology eliminates national barriers, countries which capitalise on cultural diversity have a significant advantage.

There can be few languages not spoken in Australia and few global markets that Australians have not worked in. It is the promotion of our diversity which has often been a key to our success in competitive situations, such as our successful bid for the Sydney 2000 Olympic Games. In this instance, the culturally diverse communities which helped with the bid will continue that support throughout the Games, thus ensuring that the special requirements of our overseas visitors are met.

In 1999 the National Multicultural Advisory Council report, *Australian multiculturalism for a new century: Towards inclusiveness* stated that: 'The Council believes that multicultural policies have served Australia very well, contributing to a fairer and just society. Australia, with all its cultural diversity, remains a cohesive and harmonious society, and this diversity has contributed significantly to its economic, cultural and social sophistication.'

The Council's vision for Australian multiculturalism is: 'A united and harmonious Australia, built on the foundations of our democracy and developing its continually evolving nationhood by recognising, embracing, valuing and investing in its heritage and cultural diversity.'

> English is our shared language, our lingua franca, but language is inclusive, additive. I believe in additive bilingualism, so I can speak Polish just as well as I speak English and without any tremor. I can switch from one to the other. I don't think I violate my Australian-ness by knowing another language.
> —Professor J.J. (George) Smolicz AM, Director of the Centre for Intercultural Studies and Multicultural Education, the University of Adelaide.

THE IMPACT OF MULTICULTURALISM

Food

In the recently published multimedia documentary, *Making multicultural Australia* (Board of Studies NSW), many views address the question: Is Australia a multicultural society? The discussions on food, religion and the arts indicate that there is no part of Australian life and lifestyle untouched by the impact of multiculturalism.

'Food must be the most obvious aspect of Australian multiculturalism. The revolution in Australian cuisine is one of the most notable ways in which Australia reflects the past 50 years of gathering immigrants from around the world.

'The history of Australia's changing eating habits is also a history of some migrant groups and their dispersal throughout Australia over the past century. Greeks, for example, were associated with restaurants and cafes in country towns, and in the cities, with fruit and vegetable shops, milk bars, fish shops and oyster bars, as well as with the fishing industry itself. Chinese market gardeners used to supply the fresh fruit and vegetables to many towns and cities, and, by the 1950s, Chinese restaurateurs, too, had spread around the country, offering many Australians their first taste of 'ethnic' food.

> Australia can't expect people to be of the same religion and they can't expect to be of the same biological background. We have different looks, but language we can share and food we can share.
> —Professor J.J.(George) Smolicz

'Cappuccino is the third most popular drink in Australia, after milk and soft drinks. It's hard to find an Australian who hasn't had a Chinese meal. Supermarket shelves are packed with sauce additives to turn any ingredient into an Italian, Thai or Indian meal. Shoppers no longer have to find out-of-the-way specialist delicatessens for fine cheeses and European salamis, multiple varieties of noodles and breads, sauces and spices. Most greengrocers stock fruits, vegetables and herbs unknown to the cook of 30 years ago. In the dining-out centres of most cities, restaurants drawing on cultures as diverse as African and Sri Lankan, Vietnamese and Swedish, are packed with eager customers.

'Australia's fine cuisine, with award-winning food in our best restaurants, has an international reputation as a hybrid of flavours and techniques drawn from our near and far neighbours. Increasingly, the foods of Asia and Europe are replacing the foods of England, Scotland and Ireland which formed the core of Australian cooking of the past. Even hamburgers started in the United States after having been taken there by German immigrants in the late 19th century. Indigenous foods are also starting to appear as the new Australians (those who arrived after 1788) begin to explore the diet of those who lived here for the 60,000 years or more before their arrival.

'But food, in all its variety, is as much about community as cuisine. It is in the preparation or the customs associated with traditional foods that cultures are in part transmitted. Some foods are prepared by women, others by men, some foods are blessed by priests, some by the head of the household. When families come together to partake of food on special occasions like Christmas, or the celebration of the end of the Muslim fast of Ramadan or Jewish New Year or the Serbian Orthodox 'slava', they are demonstrating something about society and culture which is much more than simply about food as sustenance.'

Religion

Until the huge migrant intake after World War II, European Australians were roughly evenly divided between Catholic and Protestant Christians, reflecting, in part, the Irish and British components of the population. This meant there was no established religion, as neither Catholics nor Protestants had a substantial majority. This desire for order and balance between Protestant and Catholic had its curious side-effects: Jews, for example, were not barred in Australia from public office and a Jewish person, Lionel Samson, sat in the Western Australian Parliament nine years before one sat in the 'mother of parliaments' at Westminster.

Since Australian law is the same as British law, Judeo-Christian morality passed into secular society. The almost universal use of the (Protestant) King James version of the Bible, and its literary cousin the (Catholic) Douay-Rheims Bible, meant most English-speaking Australians had a shared reference of story, history, language and literature.

The Australian religious landscape is now very different with 80 different faiths practised. European Catholics brought changes to Anglo, or Irish Catholic, liturgy and practice, but probably the greatest changes the Church has seen have been brought about by the influx of Catholics from the Philippines, Latin America and Vietnam, as well as the Chinese from a number of Asian nations. The influx has pushed the Catholic Church's membership numbers way past those of the Anglican Church. Pacific Islanders and Koreans have greatly boosted the numbers worshipping in Protestant churches and brought new forms of worship to staunchly Anglo-Celtic traditions.

At the same time, Buddhism, Hinduism and Islam are growing apace, the growth coming not just from immigration but increasingly from the broader population. High-profile mosques and temples have become very prominent parts of city landscapes, adding a very physical element to the fast-changing face of Australian religious adherence. Even the Jewish community, which has played a significant role in the development of all aspects of Australian society, is being changed by immigration. Significant numbers of Jews from Russia and other parts of the old Soviet Union are introducing a new element into that community.

As a dimension of ethnicity, religion, for many immigrant groups, plays a role far greater than it does for longer-settled Australians. Thus there seems to be a lag in the secularisation of ethnic groups related to their generation of 'Australian-ness'. For example, first-generation migrants built churches and retained the customs and ceremonials of their faith; their grandchildren are much more likely to marry Australians of other faith traditions.

> Some people don't seem to understand that bilingualism is not negative to English. Often through strengthening your home language you enter English with a much firmer footing. Literacy should be acquired through understanding a language than through speaking it and then reading it and writing it. Reading and writing in English before you speak well is not advisable; it must be phased in in the right way.
> —Professor J.J. (George) Smolicz

The Arts

Australia's idea of performance and art has been transformed by immigration, with an extraordinary diversity and cross-fertilisation of approaches. Circus Oz, for example, studies with Chinese circus performers to bring a unique, animal-free circus to audiences around the world, and it is described as quintessentially Australian.

All around Australia, after school hours and on weekends, children from a multitude of cultures learn the dances, songs and music of their families' traditions, and some of them carry their enthusiasm into adulthood. It is in these expressive arts that many people find their cultural identity, and the variety of these traditions, as well as the cross-cultural hybrids which are emerging, are altering our concept of Australian culture in the visual and performing arts.

> Wherever I go in Europe, people often ask, 'Where do you come from?' I answer, 'I'm Australian.' Very often their reply is, 'You don't look Australian. Are you sure?' You never know what to say to that. Do you say, 'Look, I was just joking about that Australian business; I am actually Japanese', or something like that? That goes to the heart of the identity crisis. What does an Australian look like?
> —Jason Yat-sen Li

The Media

Changes in the Australian electronic media have helped reflect the changing nature of multicultural Australia. Early services were dominated by the ABC, styled on the traditions of the BBC and presenting an essentially monocultural Australia. Commercial services reinforced this image with an injection of popular US and US-modelled programming. During the 1970s, in the face of demands from the increasingly influential ethnic communities, particularly in Sydney and Melbourne, the government began to support ethnic radio, and then ethnic television. The Special Broadcasting Service (SBS) was established, its origins being in the experimental radio stations 2EA and 3EA, which began in 1975 with limited non-English language services in Sydney and Melbourne. SBS's multicultural television service started in 1989 with limited broadcasts in the same cities. Not only is it a service that's still the only one of its kind in the world, in its more than 20 years' lifetime SBS has helped redefine Australia to itself, and now other broadcasters have begun to more accurately portray the real Australia, with its many different faces, colours and accents.

> I think therein lies the heart of the identity crisis for immigrants, particularly immigrants who look different, who don't fit into the stereotype of what an Australian is meant to look like. The beefy, blond guy in the Chesty Bond singlet, or the bronzed Lifesaver at Bondi? If you don't fit that image you do suffer a bit of an identity crisis.
> —Jason Yat-sen Li

DOES MULTICULTURALISM LEAD TO ETHNIC CONFLICT?

The Australian model of multiculturalism is unique, and there is no evidence that ethnic conflict has resulted. In fact, the remarkable thing about Australia has been how the public policies of multiculturalism have helped prevent long-held overseas hostilities being re-fought on different terrain.

During the 1991 Gulf War, the Sydney Jewish newspaper, *The Australian Jewish News*, was one of the first media to speak out against the harassment of Sydney's Muslims; when Adelaide's old Jewish cemetery was cruelly vandalised, the local Muslim community was one of the first to express its anger and concern. When the former Yugoslavia began to disintegrate and generate bitter ethnic conflict, Australian Serb, Croat and Muslim community leaders worked together to promote harmony and understanding among their local community members.

Traditional 'homeland' tensions are not always left behind – people cannot easily abandon their histories and deepest concerns – and they do erupt occasionally when precipitated by events overseas. But the social fabric of Australia remains firm through these conflicts, because control is exercised and because the structures of multiculturalism that have evolved over the past 20 years and more provide ways of resolution.

> I describe Australians as a nation of amnesiacs. People come here to forget, to start a new life, to start again. But, to what extent can you forget? To what extent can you leave behind what you are running from, or simply leaving, to give yourself a better chance, to give your family a better chance?
> —Jason Yat-sen Li

BUSINESS

Discussions about the economic aspects of immigration are of continuing interest to administrators, researchers and the public. Whether the debate is about unemployment, workforce skills or residents' income, the first point to be recognised is that in adding to the population, all areas of the economy are affected.

Immigration has played a critical role in building Australia's economy, with many examples of entrepreneurial opportunities created and developed by immigrants. Post-war immigration served the purpose of developing Australia's infrastructure and communication networks. The Snowy Mountains Hydro-electric Scheme is a fine example, where thousands of migrants from war-ravaged Europe responded to offers of work building dams, tunnels and power stations.

Face the Facts, published by the Federal Race Discrimination Commissioner (1997), states: 'Business migrants inject significant funds into the Australian economy. In 1996–1997 $856 million was transferred to the Australian economy. In 1995–1996, 4900 business migrants arrived, an increase of 4000 over 1993-1994. Surveys of business migrants have shown that, within 12 months of arrival, over half had established businesses employing an average of five staff, and around half had generated export earnings.'

In the professions, land development, retailing, manufacturing, agriculture, horticulture and technology, the newcomers have followed their dreams and taken risks. In addition to their individual successes, they have provided a constant flow of energy and innovation to Australian business.

The advantages to the Australian economy are obvious as the skills in language and culture allow Australian companies to develop new export products for homeland markets and to develop new markets for traditional Australian products. The benefit from these skills is further enhanced by the actual market knowledge and personal contacts possessed by Australians in and about their former homelands.

Cultural diversity is more than exotic cuisine, colourful national costumes and folk dancing. Few nations have achieved a history of such growth while living in peace and harmony. It is an achievement to recognise and celebrate.

Chapter Ten

The facts about us

WHAT IS THE COMPOSITION OF AUSTRALIA'S MIGRANT POPULATION?

At June 30 1995 23% of Australia's population was born overseas.

7% were born in the UK and Ireland, 6.4% were born in Europe, 4.8% in Asia, 2.1% in Oceania, 1.2% in the Middle East and Africa, and less than 2% in other regions.

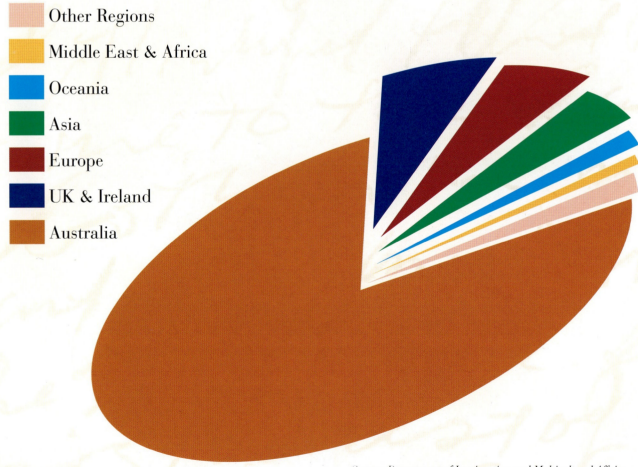

Source: Department of Immigration and Multicultural Affairs, Key Facts in Immigration Sheet No 38.

WHAT ARE THE FACTS ON OUR DIVERSITY?

Australia is a multicultural nation demographically:

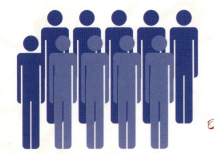

4 out of 10 Australians are migrants or the children of migrants

1 in 4 Australians was born overseas

13.7% of Australians were born overseas in non-English speaking countries

People from over 160 countries live in Australia

Source: ABS Social Trends 1996, Department of Immigration and Multicultural Affairs, Key Facts in Immigration Sheet No 15.

WHAT ARE THE CURRENT LEVELS OF IMMIGRATION?

The migrant intake changes annually. Levels of immigration have been lower in the last five years than in most years recorded since WWII.

The number of migrants who arrived in Australia in 1995–1996 was 82,500. The overall number of settlers (including refugees) arriving in the financial year of 1995–1996 was just over 99,000.

COUNTRIES OF ORIGIN

New Zealand 12.4%, the UK 11.4% and China 11.3% in 1995–1996.

Net migration closer to 60,500.

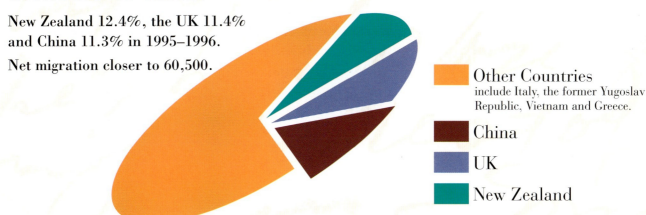

- Other Countries include Italy, the former Yugoslav Republic, Vietnam and Greece.
- China
- UK
- New Zealand

Chapter Ten – The facts about us | 165

Participants' Directory

In the past 10 years we have published over 70 books featuring Australia's achievements, whether by State, by industry or through the histories of our great corporations. We will continue to dedicate our efforts to supporting and promoting outstanding Australians who have contributed to our progress and who have seriously influenced, in their own way, the development and stature of our nation.

Perpetual is an ethnically diverse financial services company bound together by a strong commitment to client service, mutual respect and courtesy. As a workplace we are a continuing example of the principle of "a fair go".
Founded in the 1880's we have grown into a truly multicultural company, deriving enormous energy from the broad range of talents, backgrounds and perspectives of our staff.
We are proud to support the publication of this important work.

With 170,000 employees and 100 million customers in 100 countries around the world, Citigroup is synonymous with multiculturalism and ethnic diversity. As one of the world's truly global companies, we are committed to each and every one of our relationships, be they with our clients or staff. Through our many community programs and policies in countries around the world, we strive to create a climate of inclusion, where people can work and grow together, respecting each other's unique beliefs, cultures and values.

Building relationships with millions of people – from all backgrounds – to help them build wealth and realise their financial goals is the foundation for the Commonwealth Bank being the bank for all Australians. Our customers and staff have contributed greatly to our rich and diverse nation, where many dreams of a better life for our children and the future have thrived.

Participants' Directory

A WORLD OF ENTERTAINMENT.

Australia has a distinct cultural composition which embraces and celebrates our differences while rejoicing in our common bonds of being Australian. Crown takes pride in our organisation's ethnic diversity. It is our belief that it is Australia's multicultural background which is the foundation for our country's success.

Australia's society allows its people, regardless of background and beliefs, to freely develop their talents and abilities. The cultural diversity of Australian society has helped to create a very modern and accepting community. Few nations can show such an impressive record of democracy, fair treatment and harmonious relationship of people of different backgrounds as Australia.

The Ethnic Affairs Commission of New South Wales blazed a trail for other Australian states to follow more than 20 years ago, and continues to show the way. In those years it has created an environment where the bureaucracy is responsive to the needs of a culturally diverse society; where business people know that diversity needs different types of marketing, sometimes different types of products and services and that it provides the tools to create new products and reach new foreign markets; where the news media no longer behaves as if it was reporting or servicing a monoculture; and where the equality of all peoples has the recognition of all political parties and the force of law.

What Does Ford mean by Diversity?

Diversity is all the differences that make each of us a special, unique person. Ford and the unions are committed to valuing diversity. This also means allowing people to work in safe, productive environments, where individual differences are respected and valued, and where we all have the chance to reach our real potential.

Participants' Directory

QUEENSLAND GOVERNMENT

Multicultural Affairs Queensland
Department of the Premier and Cabinet

Queensland – as one of Australia's most dynamic States – has embraced the many economic, social and cultural advantages of multiculturalism. Multicultural Affairs Queensland is the State Government's lead agency implementing the Multicultural Queensland Policy across the whole of government and the wider community. It promotes multiculturalism and positive community relations to create harmony and cohesion through its grants, consultation and information programs.

SNOWY MOUNTAINS
HYDRO-ELECTRIC AUTHORITY

The Snowy Mountains Hydro-electric Scheme brought together over 100,000 people, many of them migrants from post-war Europe, to work on an epic vision which would take 25 years to complete. This astonishing human accomplishment became a focus of national pride and engineering excellence and continues to provide a proud legacy for all Australians. In the centuries to come, the Snowy will continue to supply clean, renewable hydro-electric energy and crucial water solutions for the driest inhabited continent on Earth.

As an organisation that thrives on the passion for racing and sport shared by so many diverse cultures, TAB Limited is proud to reflect the great value of ethnic diversity in both our customer relationships and our employment policies.

Index

ATKIN, Elsa
12, **19**, 30, 54, 72, 90, 106, 124

BAUM, Caroline
12, **20**, 30, 54, 72, 90, 113, 124, 138

BESLEY, Tim
12, **21**, 90, 106, 138

BLASS, Wolf
12, **22**, 38, 54, 90, 113, 124, 138

BOYATZIS, Paul
23, 30, 72, 90, 113, 124, 138

CASSAB, Judy
24-25, 30, 54, 91, 113

CASSAR, Leslie
26, 30, 74, 125, 138

CHAI, Arlene
27, 38, 54, 72, 91, 139

CHROMY, Josef
31, **40-41**, 55, 73, 92

DHARMANANDA, Mala
13, 31, **42-43**, 61, 72, 107, 125, 139

DONALDSON, Anita
12, 38, **44**, 73

GEORGIOU, Petro
32, **45**, 56, 106, 125, 152, 157

GERMANOS-KOUTSOUNADIS, Vivi
14, 33, **46-47**, 56, 73, 107, 126, 141

GOBBO, Sir James
13, 32, **48-49**, 56, 73, 92, 107, 139

GRADY, Diane
13, **50**, 73, 92, 107, 125, 139

ISOGAWA, Akira
13, 38, **51**, 56, 92, 107, 140

JEGOROW, Bill
13, 32, 56, **62**, 107, 125

JOHNSON, Ted
13, 33, 61, **63**, 107, 126, 140

KATS-CHERNIN, Elena
14, 33, **64-65**, 73, 92, 139

KERKYASHARIAN, Stepan
105, 158

KLEPAC, Lou
14, 33, 55, **66-67**, 74, 93, 108, 126

KORNER, Judit
14, 38, **68-69**, 75, 93, 109, 140

KOVACEVIC, Ilija
18, 35, 60, **78**

KUNKEL, Ted
15, 33, 74, **79**, 109, 126

LAPAINE, George
16, 34, 56, 74, **80-81**, 93, 109, 126

LE, Dai
16, 34, 74, **82-83**, 93, 109, 127, 141

LE, Tan
16, 34, 75, **84**, 93, 109, 141

LEIBLER, Mark
34, **85**, 94, 110, 127, 141

LEONG, Nelson
15, 34, 75, **86-87**, 94, 142

LI, Jason Yat-sen
157, 161, 162

LUKAS, Isabel
154, 155

MAK, Anita
18, 57, 75, **97**, 110

MURE, George
61, 75, 95, **98**, 110, 127

NANDAN, Satendra
35, 76, **99**, 110, 127, 142

NKRUMAH, Juliana
16, 35, 58, 76, 94, **100-101**, 111, 127

PARBO, Sir Arvi
38, 76, 95, **102-103**, 112, 127

RAMOS, Rolando
16, 35, 57, 76, 95, **115**, 128, 142

ROACH, Gladys
36, 58, 76, 111, **116**

ROACH, Neville
17, 58, 77, 112, **117**

RUSSO, Sarina
36, 112, **118**, 128

SANZ, Miguel
17, 39, 58, **119**, 128, 142

SARAGOSSI, Joe
59, **120**, 128

SCHMIDMAIER, Dagmar
36, 59, 96, 114, **121**, 129, 142

SCIACCA, Con
18, 114, 129, **130**

SHAHIN, Fred
36, 76, 113, **131**, 142

SIMONS, Paul
17, 114, **132-133**

SMOLICZ, J.J. (George)
158, 159, 160

SPIGELMAN, Jim
114, 129, **134**

THOMAS, Ngoc Trang
17, 36, 96, 114, 129, **135**, 143

TRAMBAS, Jim
17, 39, 59, 77, 96, 114, 129, **145**

TSZYU, Kostya
37, 60, 77, **146-147**

WHITEN, Agnes
18, 60, 77, 114, 129, **148-149**

WOLLNER, Magda
18, **150**

WU, Wilson
39, 77, 114, **151**

Bibliography

Murphy Brian, *The Other Australia – Experiences of Migration*, Cambridge University Press, 1993.

Castles Stephen, Foster William, Iredale Robyn, Withers Glen, *Immigration and Australia, Myths and Realities*, Allen & Unwin in conjunction with the Housing Industry Association Limited, 1998.

Molony John, *The Penguin Bicentennial History of Australia*, Viking Penguin Books, 1987.

Reynolds Henry, *This Whispering In Our Hearts*, Allen & Unwin, 1998.

Australian multiculturalism for a new century: Toward inclusiveness, National Multicultural Advisory Council, Department of Immigration and Multicultural Affairs, 1999.

Sandler Martin W., *Immigrants*, Library of Congress Book, Harper Collins, 1995.

Making multicultural Australia, a multimedia documentary, Board of Studies, NSW, 1999.

Viewpoints, a Collection of speeches on multicultural issues, Ethnic Affairs Commission NSW, 1996.

Australian Multicultural Foundation – various papers.

Human Rights and Equal Opportunities Commission – various papers.

Australians: A Historical Library, Fairfax Syme and Weldon Associates, 1987.

Photo Credits

Page 5 Fountain Pen Images ® copyright 1999 Photodisc, Inc.; Page 6-7 Typewriter Images ® copyright 1999 Photodisc, Inc.; page 8 Scribble Images ® copyright 1999 Photodisc, Inc.; page 9 Scribble Images ® copyright 1999 Photodisc, Inc.; page 10-11 International Photographic Library; page 12 Wallaby © Photoessentials http://www.photoessentials.com.au, Harbour Bridge, BASF Australia, Scribble Images ® copyright 1999 Photodisc, Inc.; page 13 Blue sky Images ® copyright 1999 Photodisc, Inc., Scribble Images ® copyright 1999 Photodisc, Inc.; page 14 Scribble Images ® copyright 1999 Photodisc, Inc., Toast Images ® copyright 1999 Photodisc, Inc. page 15 Scribble Images ® copyright 1999 Photodisc, Inc., Parrots Peter Walton Photography Pty Ltd; page 16-17 Lizard © Photoessentials http://www.photoessentials.com.au; page 16 Sydney © Photoessentials http://www.photoessentials.com.au, Scribble Images ® copyright 1999 Photodisc, Inc.; page 17 Scribble Images ® copyright 1999 Photodisc, Inc.; page 18 Scribble Images ® copyright 1999 Photodisc, Inc., Crocodile © Photoessentials http://www.photoessentials.com.au; page 28-29 Book in Chains, Masterfile Australia; page 30 Scribble Images ® copyright 1999 Photodisc, Inc. ; page 31 Scribble Images ® copyright 1999 Photodisc, Inc., Empty plate Images ® copyright 1999 Photodisc, Inc.; page 30 Pen in Hand Images ® copyright 1999 Photodisc, Inc.; page 32 Scribble Images ® copyright 1999 Photodisc, Inc., page 32 (top) Splash Images ® copyright 1999 Photodisc, Inc., (bottom) Surf © Photoessentials http://www.photoessentials.com.au, page 33 Scribble Images ® copyright 1999 Photodisc, Inc.; page 34 Blackboard Images ® copyright 1999 Photodisc, Inc.; Scribble Images ® copyright 1999 Photodisc, Inc.; page 35 Scribble Images ® copyright 1999 Photodisc, Inc., Tins and String Images ® copyright 1999 Photodisc, Inc.; page 36 Study Images ® copyright 1999 Photodisc, Inc., Scribble Images ® copyright 1999 Photodisc, Inc.; page 37 Scribble Images ® copyright 1999 Photodisc, Inc., TV Images ® copyright 1999 Photodisc, Inc.; page 38-39 Football/Allsport; Scribble Images ® copyright 1999 Photodisc, Inc.; page 52-53 Homesickness Superstock Australia; page 55 Clock Images ® copyright 1999 Photodisc, Inc.; page 54-55 Dead Plant in Soil, The Photo Library of Australia, Inc., Scribble Images ® copyright 1999 Photodisc, Inc.; page 56 Letters Images ® copyright 1999 Photodisc, Inc. Scribble Images ® copyright 1999 Photodisc, Inc.; page 57 Scribble Images ® copyright 1999 Photodisc, Inc., Mountains, Peter Walton Photography Pty Ltd, Inc.; page 58-59 Scribble Images ® copyright 1999 Photodisc, Inc., (bottom) Shoppers Woolworths Limited, page 58 Rice bowl Images ® copyright 1999 Photodisc, Inc.; page 59 (top) Baseball glove Images ® copyright 1999 Photodisc, Inc.; page 60-61 Scribble Images ® copyright 1999 Photodisc, Inc.; page 60 Jewellery Images ® copyright 1999 Photodisc, Inc.; page 61 Sandwich Images ® copyright 1999 Photodisc, Inc.; page 72-73 Education University of Western Australia; Scribble Images ® copyright 1999 Photodisc, Inc.; page 74 Plane Images ® copyright 1999 Photodisc, Inc.; page 74-75 Scribble Images ® copyright 1999 Photodisc, Inc.; page 75 Celebration Images ® copyright 1999 Photodisc, Inc.; page 76-77 Scribble Images ® copyright 1999 Photodisc, Inc.; page 77 Dog Images ® copyright 1999 Photodisc, Inc. page 88-89 Beach Image, International Photographic Library; page 90-91 Scribble Images ® copyright 1999 Photodisc, Inc.; page 90 Kangaroo paw © Photoessentials http://www.photoessentials.com.au; page 91 Australian landscape © Photoessentials http://www.photoessentials.com.au; page 92-93 Scribble Images ® copyright 1999 Photodisc, Inc., Dunbogan Beach © Photoessentials http://www.photoessentials.com.au; page 94-95 Scribble Images ® copyright 1999 Photodisc, Inc.; page 94 (top) Heart Images ® copyright 1999 Photodisc, Inc.; page 95 Queensland Art Gallery, Department Premier and Cabinet; page 96 Watersports © Photoessentials http://www.photoessentials.com.au, Scribble Images ® copyright 1999 Photodisc, Inc. page 104-105 Images ® copyright 1999 Photodisc, Inc.; page 106 Ethnic Affairs Commission of NSW, Scribble Images ® copyright 1999 Photodisc, Inc.; page 107 Scribble Images ® copyright 1999 Photodisc, Inc.; page 108 Scribble Images ® copyright 1999 Photodisc, Inc., Notepad Images ® copyright 1999 Photodisc, Inc.; page 109 Earth Images ® copyright 1999 Photodisc, Inc.; page 110 TV dinner Images ® copyright 1999 Photodisc, Inc., Scribble Images ® copyright 1999 Photodisc, Inc.; page 111 Scribble Images ® copyright 1999 Photodisc, Inc., Capsicums Images ® copyright 1999 Photodisc, Inc.; page 112 Scribble Images ® copyright 1999 Photodisc, Inc., Football Images ® copyright 1999 Photodisc, Inc.; page 113 Images ® copyright 1999 Photodisc, Inc.; page 114 Scribble Images ® copyright 1999 Photodisc, Inc.; Page 122-123 Travel Case and Mementos, The Photo Library of Australia, Inc.; page 124 Young at heart © Photoessentials http://www.photoessentials.com.au, Scribble Images ® copyright 1999 Photodisc, Inc.; page 125 Exotic Pine, Department of Primary Industries, Forestry, Queensland, Scribble Images ® copyright 1999 Photodisc, Inc.; page 126 Scribble Images ® copyright 1999 Photodisc, Inc.; page 127 Scribble Images ® copyright 1999 Photodisc, Inc.; page 128 NY traffic Images ® copyright 1999 Photodisc, Inc., Scribble Images ® copyright 1999 Photodisc, Inc.; page 129 Scribble Images ® copyright 1999 Photodisc, Inc.; page 136-137 Silhouette, The Photo Library of Australia; page 138 Red wine, Images ® copyright 1999 Photodisc, Inc.; Scribble Images ® copyright 1999 Photodisc, Inc.; page 139 Scribble Images ® copyright 1999 Photodisc, Inc.; page 140-141 Bridge, International Photographic Library, Inc. Scribble Images ® copyright 1999 Photodisc, Inc.; page 142 Boxing gloves Images ® copyright 1999 Photodisc, Inc. page 142 Scribble Images ® copyright 1999 Photodisc, Inc.; page 143 Scribble Images ® copyright 1999 Photodisc, Inc.; page 144 Scribble Images ® copyright 1999 Photodisc, Inc.; page 152-153 Kids, Ethnic Affairs Commission of NSW; page 154 Scribble Images ® copyright 1999 Photodisc, Inc.; page 155 Scribble Images ® copyright 1999 Photodisc, Inc., Opal Images ® copyright 1999 Photodisc, Inc. page 156 Scribble Images ® copyright 1999 Photodisc, Inc.; page 157 Scribble Images ® copyright 1999 Photodisc, Inc.; page 158 Scribble Images ® copyright 1999 Photodisc, Inc.; page 159 Scribble Images ® copyright 1999 Photodisc, Inc.; page 160 Scribble Images ® copyright 1999 Photodisc, Inc.; page 161 Scribble Images ® copyright 1999 Photodisc, Inc.; page 162 Scribble Images ® copyright 1999 Photodisc, Inc.; page 163 Scribble Images ® copyright 1999 Photodisc, Inc.; page 164 Scribble Images ® copyright 1999 Photodisc, Inc.; page 165 Scribble Images ® copyright 1999 Photodisc, Inc.

Images of the Certificate of Citizenship and the Commonwealth Coat of Arms used with permission of the Australian Government.